C000165380

Praise for *The Up To No Gc*

"It takes courage to step out of you.. ....
daring. Like a true BFF, Jane Wilson shares fun and actionable
steps so you can channel your inner diva, embrace your body,
and step into confidence to get your groove back."

CHALENE JOHNSON *New York Times*-bestselling author; health, business, and lifestyle expert; founder, SmartLife; top health podcaster

"A delicious, sassy, and enlightening guide to liberate your
inner rock star!"

SUSAN SANDLER theatrical speaker, clarity strategist, and author

"While the judgy neighbour next door might call it 'no good,'
I can tell you from firsthand experience that Jane Wilson's
approach to life is good science, good fun, and good for
you. This book has me excited about joining the Up To No
Good Club!"

LIANE DAVEY *New York Times*-bestselling author of *The Good Fight*

"This book is for anyone who has ever struggled with being true
to their heart. So many societal constructs exist for women
around what it means to be authentic, bold, beautiful, sexy,
and confident. Jane Wilson deconstructs those concepts and
provides a framework for building your stories and identities
according to your own rule book. A truly unique story with
inspiring lessons for women of all ages, *The Up To No Good
Club* is a must-read."

KATIE SOY storyteller and author of *The Firefly and the Storm*

"There are so many books about improving your life, but so few that become powerful guides that you refer to time and again. Jane Wilson's book is one of the latter. Women all over the world will see themselves in these stories. This is a real, fun, and empowering read that will transform how you see yourself!"

JEN STILLION speaker and movement coach

"Uplifting and encouraging! Jane puts the 'POW!' in personal empowerment! The combination of practical tips and tools with the personal stories of challenges overcome and confidence reclaimed kept me enthralled! Enjoyed every page!"

MARCI WARHAFT author of *The Good Stripper: A Soccer Mom's Memoir of Lies, Loss and Lapdances*

"One of the most important gifts a woman can give herself is to be fully present. It allows you to hold your space in life. Jane Wilson has influenced many women with her passion for pole dancing to create a sense of presence. A woman's gifts appear at the highest level during this state. I so appreciate how Jane speaks her truth to help others find their truth. There is nothing better than hearing one's powerful voice. Well done!"

ELLEN LATHAM MS, creator and cofounder, Orangetheory Fitness

"*The Up To No Good Club: Defining Your Life with Strength and Swagger* is wonderfully relatable with a dash of spice. This book provides a unique spin on how to live your best life! As a pole dance instructor myself, I was delighted to see the author reveal life lessons discovered through pole dance. If you're looking to find the fire within you, this book is a must."

JULIE BRAND founder, Studioveena.com

"Jane Wilson is a light that shines so bright—this book immediately made me feel as if I was sitting next to her. Her raw, authentic, and honest book looks at life, motherhood, being a woman, and showing up! Damn, she brought me to tears and then made me laugh and pause to dive into what part I saw in myself. Thank you for honouring women and our journey!"

MELISSA JOY OLSON founder and CEO, Euphoria Studio, Frenchtown, NJ

"*The Up To No Good Club* brought me to places I didn't expect. It made me feel happy and sad. It reminded me that life is precious, that every day we need to not only be grateful for what we have, but also to not shy away from living our lives fully, authentically, and without shame. The exercises at the end of each chapter were thoughtful and self-reflective in a great way. I highly recommend this book for anyone who feels stuck or afraid to live their life on their own terms."

ELISABETH MAGALHAES director, Canadian Pole Fitness Association

"If you have a strong reaction to the word 'sexy' (good or bad)—you need to read this book! If you're stuck in a rut, *The Up To No Good Club* is the answer. Jane Wilson's journey is so relatable; she gives hope to anyone struggling with anxiety, comparison, and the feeling of 'is this it?' about our lives. *The Up To No Good Club* is a beautiful reminder to live life on your own terms. If you feel like it's too late to make a change in your life, you need to read this book. Part storytelling, part how-to, this is the ultimate guide to getting your groove back!"

NATALIE BORCH owner, The Pink Studio Dance + Fitness and body confidence expert

"A strong, sassy, sophisticated, and relatable memoir! While you may have never danced in Dita Von Teese's Burlesque show, Jane Wilson's storytelling style quickly draws you into her world and into her high heels. Every woman can easily connect with the emotions she shares through the peaks and valleys of her life—so many 'me too!' moments!"

ELLIE PARVIN communication expert and educator

The
UP TO
NO GOOD
CLUB

The
UP TO
NO GOOD
CLUB

Defining Your Life
with Strength and Swagger

JANE WILSON

Foreword by Michelle Mynx

Up To No Good
PRESS

ISBN 978-1-77771-140-5 (paperback)
ISBN 978-1-77771-141-2 (ebook)

Published by Up To No Good Press
janewilson.com

Produced by Page Two
pagetwo.com

Edited by Emily Schultz
Copyedited by John Sweet
Proofread by Alison Strobel
Cover design by Taysia Louie
Cover illustrations by Nikkie Stinchcombe
Interior design by Setareh Ashrafologhalai

janewilson.com

Dedicated to my Mother.
If life had dealt you a different
hand, you would have led
the Up To No Good Club.

CONTENTS

FOREWORD

AS I REACHED for my pre-show Bellini at the Gladstone Hotel bar, a voice sang behind me.

"Excuse me, Michelle Mynx? It's so good to meet you. I'm performing pole in this show too. Just like you, eh?"

Immediately intrigued and delighted by the cheerful Canadian accent, I turned to a bubbly little redhead grinning from ear to ear. Before I could stop her, she reached into her purse and pulled out those colourful bills to pay for my drink.

I was performing in the Toronto Burlesque Festival, with my pole partner, Katrina Dohl, as the burlesque pole dancing duo known as Gravity Plays Favorites. To the best of our knowledge, Katie and I were the only pole dancers in the burlesque scene. Then we met and fell in love with this polite little paradox of a person—a pole dancing, burlesque-performing hockey mom.

This began our friendship with Jane.

Charmed by our outward differences, I discovered just how alike we were in many ways. I'm an American outspoken queer feminist—mom only to the furry and scaled. My entrance into pole dancing started as a stripper. I found strength and power in this newly discovered ownership and agency over my own body and sexual expression. Pole quickly became my favourite part of the job. Being a career dancer for 15 years, I segued my love of this incredible art form into a life of teaching as a successful studio owner.

Jane was a preschool teacher, a suburban wife and mother, living the heteronormative Canadian dream. Her entrance to the world of pole was through taking lessons as a way to feel sexy, and it ended up changing her life. Her perspective grew from a path of self-discovery, much the same as many of our students, while mine began from the origins of modern pole dance—the strip club. Yet our passion for the magic of pole dance, and our desire to share it with anyone who wishes to learn, was much the same. (Along with our mutual love for '80s music, the deliciously bad movie *Showgirls*, and late-night giggles while drinking moonshine!)

Throughout our journeys, Jane and I have taught thousands of people—especially women and femmes—to embrace their inner badass and discover their own authentic brand of sensuality combined with strength; to be brave enough to suck at something new, to dedicate time for themselves, to have the courage to be heard and take up the space we are all worthy of in this life.

Despite the vast differences in our lives and life perspectives, we ALL have so much more in common than we can imagine. Reading this book is like listening to a wise friend who doesn't judge or shame, but allows you to make mistakes, to feel sad, overwhelmed, or maybe even helpless. As I devoured each page, I laughed out loud and wiped tears as I related to the heart-wrenching tales. She feeds encouragement with directions on turning your own life around.

At first, this book allows you to feel seen and your emotions validated, then leaves you motivated and inspired—excited about doing the prompts in each chapter. It teaches you to be proud of your rebelliousness and face your flaws with confidence and everlasting hope.

Caution: Side effects may include walking into a pole studio and falling in love with yourself.

MICHELLE MYNX, owner and founder of Mynx Academy of Pole Dance; producer of the Mynx Pole Dance Extravaganza; cofounder of Gravity Plays Favorites, St. Louis, Missouri

Instagram: @MichelleMynx

Facebook: Michelle Mynx / Michelle Mynx Academy of Pole Dance

YouTube: Michelle Mynx

INTRODUCTION

NEVER IMAGINED I'd create a space for people to reinvent themselves—a decade of hair-tossing, pole-climbing, heel-banging mayhem, where over 10,000 people explored their strength and sexiness and increased their confidence. Being witness to people's transformations is a joy and an honour that I hold with respect. How magical an experience to see someone who is shy and uncertain start to flourish and develop fire with a take-no-prisoners view on life. Their ability to motivate grows, and soon they handle any obstacle in their life with grace. I admire it so much. Seeing that change in others was my main objective when I created my pole dancing studio.

Reinvention can be scary.

Reinvention requires bravery.

Reinvention calls us to have faith and honour the process of change.

Reinvention takes us down a new path where we come out the other side with more strength and courage than we had before.

I have redefined myself before, when I said goodbye to crayons, fingerpaints, singing songs, and reading stories for toddlers in my childcare classroom. Would you believe that my original career path was as a preschool teacher during the day and, in the evening, a college instructor who taught Child Development and Creative Learning Environment courses for the Early Childhood Education program? After 10 years, I quit my career with absolutely no safety net, survived the leap, and became a pole dancing studio owner. I'm all about life pivots and reinventions.

My pivot to the pole started with an indignant response to a recommendation. Six months after quitting my job as a preschool teacher, while our toddlers dug in the sandbox, I shared with my friend how I had recently been feeling bored. I wanted a non-"mom-like" activity—something fun, that didn't involve crayons and Gymboree. I was thinking Jazzercise or maybe a book club. Angie had a different idea.

"Hey! Take pole dancing classes! A new place opened up downtown," Angie blurted.

"What? A pole dancing place? You know that's called a strip club!" I scrunched up my nose, as though I smelled something disgusting.

Flicking her shovel to toss some sand in my direction, Angie corrected me. "No. It's a place with poles and they teach you how to do the stuff the dancers do. I wanna try! You in? Actually, don't answer. You are in. I'll pay for it."

Rolling my eyes, I puffed with resignation. "I gotta see this to believe it."

Three days later, wearing an oversized sweatshirt I pulled from the laundry basket, sweatpants, and running shoes, I stood in a 1,000-square-foot room with hot-pink walls and 10 gleaming poles. At the front of the room stood a petite blonde wearing black spaghetti-strap leotards and a long black flowy mesh skirt. As the instructor reached over to the stereo, she glanced at my footwear and softly informed me, "Oh, honey, you won't need running shoes in a pole class. Just go barefoot, and one day you'll wear heels," and then she flipped the switch to play the CD.

As the music began, I scrambled to take off my running shoes and socks, placing them at the pole I was directed to stand beside.

"Honey, you're gonna need to move your shoes and socks, or you'll trip when we start strutting around the pole." She giggled as her hips swayed to begin the class warm-up.

The words "strut around the pole" stuck in my mind. What could that possibly mean? Within minutes, the answer was revealed as the instructor seductively stepped around the pole, her hips swaying from side to side as she dragged her toes across the floor. Hesitantly, I looked over at Angie, who was "strutting" around the pole with a big grin on her face. I reached for the pole, thinking, *How does one walk around a pole? Is it the same as walking down the street?*

As though she read my mind, the instructor called out, "Lift your heels up and walk on the balls of your feet. You'll be able to pivot, which makes your hips move."

She was right. Like magic, the moment I lifted my heels and started pivoting, my hips lyrically rolled to the side and my brain lit up with, *Ooooh, I like this.*

In a flash, the hour went by. Since it was years since I had intentionally worked out, the muscles in my arms couldn't lift my body; all I could do was strut around the pole. But I was okay with that. I had a pretty good strut, and I was hooked. At the end of the class, with a "take my money" smile, I whipped out my credit card and signed up for beginner classes.

My obsession with pole had begun. I would take class after class—learning move after move, becoming stronger every single time. After six months of being a student, I decided to fully invest in pole dancing: I would open my own location.

(Sidebar: I cringe at my arrogance when I remember how I initially felt about pole dancing. When I look back at my first reaction, I wish I hadn't been so judgmental. After that pole class, I realized how important it is to recognize the roots of pole; removing the stigma requires highlighting the exotic dance industry that brought pole to our world. Stripper shaming has no place in my life. Strippers and exotic dancers are highly stigmatized and discriminated against. Allow me to be clear: I fully support sex workers' rights, especially with regards to safety and body autonomy.)

As I made my move into this new career, the quest for a commercial space began, resulting in my being rejected more than 10 times by property owners. No one would rent to me because they believed I was going to bring in a strip club or even run a brothel in my hometown of Oakville, Ontario, Canada. One landlord accused me of not being the business owner at all, but a "front person to a prostitution ring." (Well, hello there, stigma.) At the time, pole dancing wasn't yet mainstream; it hadn't turned into the industry it is today. In fact, it was taboo. Jennifer Lopez and Shakira hadn't shaken their fringe-covered bodies on the Super Bowl stage in front of 103 million viewers, with J.Lo on the pole, backlit with her arms raised to the air, showcasing pole on a national stage. This half-time show ignited a social media frenzy about appropriateness and some 1,300 FCC complaints. Yes, even in 2020, the debate over how a woman moves her body continued.

The bricks-and-mortar location for PoleFit Nation wound up being a desperate, last-ditch Hail Mary pass. After facing another "no" spiced with ridicule and an accusation of operating an illegal business, I sat in my car, waiting at the stoplight. My eyes burning with tears, and thoughts of giving up running through my mind, I looked over at an empty corner storefront space with a For Rent sign in the window.

Staring at the phone number, I contemplated calling it. However, the voice of resignation sighed in my head. *Why bother? It'll be another no. It's too hard to rent space in this town.*

As I waited for the light to turn green, I wrestled with my decision. Do I make one last phone call to see if the space is available? Or... do I keep on driving?

The light turned green.

Pressing my foot down on the accelerator, I started to drive past the space with the For Rent sign.

Halfway down the street, my gut screamed out, *Nooo!* I quickly yanked the steering wheel, making a reckless U-turn. Deep inside me, I knew I couldn't just drive away. I had to make one more phone call.

At the other end of the line was a male voice with a heavy accent. "Hello. What do you want?" he demanded.

I stuttered. "Um... Is... is this space still available to rent?"

"What do you want it for?" he barked.

My gut knotted as I prepared for the familiar shiv at my inner hope. Rejection was just a second away.

"I—I want to run a pole dancing studio in this space," I stammered. A buzzing feeling started in my fingers and crept up my arms as my face grew flushed. *Here we go again.*

I was met with silence. Then a cough. A burning sensation flooded my eyes.

"Hello? Is anyone there?" I squeezed my eyes, a tear slowly escaping under my lid.

"Yes," he said gruffly. "I'll be right there. You wait and I'll bring the papers."

My hand grabbed my chest as my heart skipped a beat. *Holy smokes! Does "papers" mean lease agreement?* I thought as I put the phone down and grabbed my compact to fix my face.

Sure enough, 15 minutes later, a beaten-up Jeep pulled up in front of the corner unit and an older gentleman stepped out, wearing a grey three-piece tweed suit with a red pocket square and a black fedora. He looked as though he was ready for a Sunday church service on a Wednesday afternoon. In his hand was a single piece of paper.

"Are you the one who called?" He squinted his eyes, looking me up and down.

Pulling my shoulders back, lifting my chin so I could meet his gaze, I replied with the sweetest smile on my face, "I sure am!"

"What are you renting the space for?" He raised his eyebrows.

Oh God ... He hadn't heard me the first time. Here goes nothing.

With a "fake it till you make it" grin, I proclaimed, "I want to open a pole dancing studio and teach people how to pole dance." A sense of pride filled my heart as I heard myself say those words. Yes, this is what I wanted to do.

He leaned forward, turning his ear to me, and said, "Pardon? A what?"

Daaaaamn.

Shrinking back, I stammered, "A p-p-pole dancing studio."

Leaning back, he let a chuckle escape while a big grin spread across his face, revealing his gold tooth. "Okay, here's the lease agreement. I'll even knock off $50. Sign it."

Are you freaking kidding me? No background check? No questioning me? Just "here's your lease"?! I looked around for a hidden camera.

"I need a pen," I responded, frantically searching my purse so I could scribble my signature on that single piece of paper before he changed his mind.

Opening up his suit jacket, he pulled out a black Waterman pen.

Just like that, standing outside the empty corner storefront space at 393 Kerr Street, without even seeing the inside of the building, I signed my lease agreement and found my studio space. My pole dancing career had begun.

Two weeks later, I found out why leasing the space had felt like a dream come true.

My landlord, who was hard of hearing, misunderstood and thought I said "ballroom dancing studio." When he was a teenager, he took up ballroom dancing and loved it, so he was excited that the space would be a future ballroom dancing studio. He knocked off $50 so he could take classes. Needless to say, he was shocked when the poles went up and I had to explain to him in more detail about pole dancing. Thankfully, his response was, "Just pay your rent." (I always did.)

FROM THAT moment on, for the next 11 years, I witnessed reinvention after reinvention. This space was more than just a location for fitness classes. A pole dancing studio is a magical place of fantasy and rebirth, where every single person, regardless of their ability, feels like the hero in their own story. It's a real-life version of *Cheers*, except instead of a bar, this is a place of brass poles, and your instructor is like Sam Malone, who welcomes you as you enter a room where "everybody knows your name." For the many years I led a pole dancing studio, people from all walks of life would bravely join in, from the 20-year-old female university student who loved to dance to K-Pop to the 73-year-old man who wanted to test his strength and feel young again. Many people assume students take pole dancing classes to satisfy their partner, but most of my students came for themselves—to spice up their workouts, build self-confidence, and feel sexy (sure), and sometimes even for personal therapy.

There was Sarah, 36 years old, who discovered sexy texts on her husband's cell—which did not come from her phone.

She was devastated by this reveal and plunged into the depths of fury. The sender of the texts was a younger woman, who Sarah believed was prettier than her. With the support of her family and friends, she left her husband (he was such a jackass) and rebuilt her self-esteem. She told me, "I stayed in bed for months. The anger was too much to bear. It was swallowing me up and stopping me from moving forward. I needed help, but shame kept me from asking. It took my best friend to step in. She practically did an intervention and encouraged me to see a therapist. While in therapy, I realized I needed 'dedicated time for me.' From there, I told my parents that I was a mess. So, they'd watch my kids while I went to pole class. This was the turning point, and I felt like a phoenix rising from the ashes. I even put a phoenix image for phone wallpaper, as a reminder."

Then there was John, a septuagenarian, whose Zumba classes were cancelled at the seniors' centre. One day, walking past the studio, he saw the poles and said, "Why not? It's still dance!" He signed up for one private lesson, and at the end announced his intention to begin his weekly pole training instead of finding a new Zumba program.

And then there was Jennifer, 39 years old, who grew up hating sports and exercise. As a kid in gym class, she would always fall and hurt herself, so she associated movement with pain—cuts, scrapes, and bruises. It was safer to sit around and watch from the sidelines. She had never worked out in her adult years. Running brought fear of tripping and falling down. Swimming involved walking around the pool and moving her arms. The word "athlete" would never have been used to describe her, until the day she started exploring her strength, and began to gain courage and the faith that exercise wasn't going to leave her on crutches. Little by little, over time, she created a new version of herself, and eventually she became an athlete by showing up at her training sessions. She dared herself to do a half marathon, "even if I end up walking it—at least I did it! I made it to the end like an athlete!"

Oh, the shows we'd put on! There were fashion shows, and pole and burlesque events with special guest performers such as Boylesque TO, an award-winning Canadian all-male burlesque troupe. These events offered opportunities for members of the studio to be seen and cheered on. I felt like a modern-day Mickey Rooney from the 1939 movie *Babes in Arms,* exclaiming to our students in class, "Hey! You know what we need to do? Let's put on a show!" Students and instructors would choreograph performances, design costumes, and invite their friends to our events. We'd play out our fantasy as performers, wearing our sequins and our false lashes, lips reddened, dancing on our chairs and poles as our guests cheered us on.

For years, although everyone else was happy, I was secretly fighting the battle of burnout. A feeling of exhaustion was seeping in, which of course totally went against the fun and spontaneous spirit of dancing. Perhaps I felt burdened by the bricks-and-mortar aspects of the space, by a sense that the four walls were holding me in? Or was it the constant "come join our studio" new student promotion that's required to maintain a fitness business? The day-to-day studio-owner pressure—making sure rent, bills, and instructors were paid—was weighing me down. Usually, I could shake it off, but it was becoming harder to keep at bay. Along with this quagmire, a little voice inside my head was telling me it was time to let the space go. At first I fought this voice, shoving it aside. Everyone was having fun, and I didn't want to upset the festivities. But the voice grew louder and louder, saying, "It's time to rest and then play a new role in people's lives." Finally, one morning at 4 a.m., I woke up with my head on a pillow that was soaked with tears, after a dream of saying goodbye. In the dream, everyone was joyous, doing their kick-ass pole ninja moves. I was watching them from the back of the room. With a smile and a sense of accomplishment, I turned and walked outside, where I was filled with sunlight and blue skies. I felt complete.

I woke up with the kind of ugly, gut-wrenching sob that is never flattering to observe. I knew in my heart that it was time to let go of the studio that I had built from scratch. I made the bold and unexpected move of selling my studio.

A new role was waiting for me, one that involved sharing stories and ideas, cheering people on, encouraging them to keep doing their best. My work as a studio owner was done, and it was time to reinvent myself again. I realized that, through the process of teaching 10,000 people, I had experienced how people create their lives to be strong, sexy, and confident, and I wanted to share that knowledge with the world. Truth is, not everyone wants to join a pole dancing studio, but many want to feel confident and have swagger in their everyday lives.

And that's where this book comes in.

Through this whole experience, I found that when we listen to our inner voice, we create an accelerating force that will dare us to break rules, bust our fears, and create the life we have always wanted. That energy propels us into a new life path, one where we are stronger and more confident; we deepen our relationships.

The net always appears. We are the hero in our story.

Shall we reshape our lives together?

Here we go.

— 1 —

WHEN THE #BESTLIFE IS NOT SO #BESTLIFE

ATHER AROUND my kitchen table, which is all decked out with my mother's vintage 1960s Rosenthal tea set and Lipton's Earl Grey steeping in the pot for us. I feel fancy sipping affordable tea from expensive fine bone china.

The first item on the agenda is to discuss the current state of affairs.

You imagined your life would be filled with ease as you bounced out of bed *before* the buzz of your alarm, a big smile on your blemish-free face. You have tons of time to apply your makeup; eyeliner is pro-level "cat-eyed" and lashes are on point. Dressed in the current fashions and driving the cleanest car, your jaunt to work consists of all green lights, a full tank of gas, and no traffic obstacles on the way to your destination. Calm mind, perfect body, not a hair out of place, and blue skies surrounding your existence, with your favourite tunes playing through your car speaker. You are living your #bestlife.

Instead, you wake up with a panicked jolt because you forgot to set the alarm.

Now you are frantic. You grab yesterday's shirt off the floor (it's okay to wear it again because you spent the day hiding from the outside world). No time to properly wash your face, just slap on some concealer because it's your best friend and will cover up yesterday's mascara smudges. Attempting to apply eyeliner, your shaky hand smears an uneven line across your lid.

You miss the pre–rush hour bliss, and now you're stuck in stop-and-go traffic, wondering how many drops of gas are left, because yesterday it was slightly hovering at the *E*.

Gripping the steering wheel, you feel sweat beginning to emerge in the armpits of your shirt. You make a mental note to visit the bathroom as soon as you arrive and use the hand dryer to evaporate the moisture from yesterday's blouse. Today, you better keep your elbows close to your body to hide those wet marks.

It freakin' sucks.

At one time, you had the world in the palm of your hand. Daydreaming as you strolled through markets, latte in hand, you were full of optimism and a take-no-prisoners mindset for the days ahead. You literally felt you could conquer anything that came your way.

But something happened.

Somehow there was a change, and now "life's responsibilities" have splashed all over you, like a massive wave enveloping you and pulling you down in its undertow. All those bills and deadlines, your overextended expectations, have gut-punched those latte-fuelled daydreams, landing you on the mat of disappointment. Even though you are making some kind of income, in a career that seems to be what you wanted, life doesn't match what you had imagined.

Where's the sense of fulfillment you thought you would feel?

You lack interest in what you once found thrilling, those plans and dreams that brought you a feeling of excitement. Now you end up spending your nights on the couch, munching on saltines because you are so damn exhausted and the latest season of *Real Housewives of Beverly Hills* has been released on Prime. Their superficial shenanigans, while they tout their collections of Louboutins and Hermès bags, are next-level dysfunction. Their trivial squabbles about who may or may not have said something are delightful, and you binge-watch their extravagance, shade, and surgical enhancements vicariously. Meanwhile, you can't seem to figure out what should be your first step towards achieving your goals. Everything makes you feel as if you are drowning, sinking further into your shows, nighttime snacking, and Facebook scrolling, because those activities feel like the better course of action for the moment. You'll get to your dreams... eventually.

There was a time when working out felt great and easy to do, but now the gym seems loaded with germs, so you'll skip it and put the membership on hold? Let's be honest, it's been a long time since you worked out, and your Lululemons are simply a fashion choice now.

I want you to know—I've been there.

For me, it was a career where I thought I was happy but deep down I was bored. I was living in a house that looked like it belonged on an episode of *Hoarders*, while I pretended that the piles of papers (a.k.a. bills) and laundry didn't exist. My eyes would glaze over the piles as I zigzagged from room to room, tiptoeing around The Stuff that I no longer saw because I was so used to it. The weight of clutter pushed me down deeper into the seat cushions, giving the couch a special magnetism.

At 30 years of age, I believed I was old.

Every New Year's Eve, as I watched the ball drop on TV, I felt this sense of impending doom in my heart. *Don't worry,* I'd tell myself, *this year will pass too, just like the rest of them. You'll survive.* I felt bloated with apathy, struggling to balance being a preschool teacher, taking care of my two young boys, and being a wife, a mother, and a daughter. Dragging myself to the "Friday finish line," embattled and exhausted, I crossed off the days until the weekend arrived. TGIF! (Or even better when it was a three-day holiday weekend.)

With the emergence of social media, I would lose myself in surfing the Web and peering into other people's lives via Facebook, while I disconnected from my husband. My friends always seemed to have the better house, with a newly renovated kitchen. And damn it, they are going on *another* vacation. (*Oh, come on. Where do they find the time or money? How is this fair?*)

Deep down inside me, I knew that life wasn't supposed to be this way.

Life was meant to be exciting and enjoyable! I started to yearn to feel inspired. To find joy throughout the day.

I longed to feel as young as my chronological age (let's be honest, feeling old at 30 is kinda sad), and I didn't want to feel hatred towards happy people anymore. I wanted to feel happy too. I wanted to jump into their bliss and ability to find humour when faced with difficulties and be a cheerleader in other people's lives.

And so it began for me, my quest to change my life.

Don't Run from Everything

This accelerating force inside me was pushing me to break rules, puncture the stagnation, and create a life that I loved.

I didn't want to leave my husband, children, or home. Running away from my current existence, enacting my own version of *The Great Escape*, wouldn't be a solution. My issues, fears, and deep-down disappointment would run after me, chasing and screaming out, "You can't run and hide from us! We'll still be there!" No, I realized I had to stand up to my demons—giving that Clint Eastwood stare at the Good, Bad, and Ugly sides of me. My fears, habits, and bullshit stories in my head were keeping me from being responsible, taking action, and feeling self-pride. To become the person I always wanted to be, so my family life would improve, I needed to put myself in the starting block, hold the runner's stance, and burst towards the life we deserved.

While change didn't happen overnight, it did materialize. The sprint became a marathon of two steps forward, one stumble back, propelling forward with little wins along the way. I took day-to-day action to feel good again. I am here to share with you the steps I took to move from hangry-eating cold spaghetti in a cluttered, hurried, and harried world to living a hair-tossing, sparkly Swarovski–fuelled, energized life.

For over five years now, I've been standing on the other side of the journey, seeing the signs of resignation that indicate we are "settling" in life. When I refer to "we," I mean people of all genders, not just women. Instead of designing our lives so we feel confident in our abilities and excited about each day, we have given up to the feeling of powerlessness and the results of our inaction. The results show in how we carry ourselves—in our voice and how we look down when asked about our day. It appears in how we refer to other people's lives, the negativity and resentment that rise up as we talk about a friend who posted a cute Instagram picture of their new outfit. The bingeing, escaping, comparing, and shutting down have robbed us of the chance of living that #bestlife.

It's time that we stop, create a plan, and become kinder to ourselves. We deserve to have a life of joy and excitement, one where we jump out of bed, knowing that our confidence and faith in our abilities will help us handle the obstacles that will come our way.

Pole Spins, Booty Shorts, and Glinda the Good Witch

In this book, along with my own story, I will share the stories of many people who have taken charge of their lives, making decisions based on what lifted and inspired them. These are folks I met during my last decade owning my pole fitness studio.

Now, if you skipped my introduction and jumped straight in, you are probably scratching your head about now, thinking, *Didn't she say she was a preschool teacher? What does she mean about pole dancing?*

It's a part of my story on how I changed my life's trajectory—the big, bold decision that had a domino effect. Now, you don't have to start pole dancing to make your life better and happier (it is fun, though). My journey to the pole is important for you to know about because it is pretty much the crux of my life. It led me to work with more than 10,000 people, helping them to become confident, strong, and inspired in life, and now I am sharing our adventures with you.

I witnessed reinventions from timid to bold, where the shy silenced their self-doubts, believed in their capabilities, and found their sassiness. I have worked with people of many ages, including teaching an 80-year-old woman how to walk around the pole (she LOVED it), and I was able to help a blind woman who yearned to feel the air flow through her hair as she took a spin. I've shown a young man how to strut in his brand new, five-inch, glittery, hot-pink Pleaser Bordellos.

Being in this world of poles, booty shorts, platform heels, and "naughty" music gave me a new perspective on boldness and mischievousness, which I want to share with you. Therefore, think of me as a variation on Glinda the Good Witch, the most powerful sorceress in the Land of Oz, who shares her knowledge in order to guide Dorothy through her adventure. Wearing the pink satin dress with the sheer overlay of silver stars, I'll wave my wand to guide you on your Yellow Brick Road of Adventure and finding your way home to yourself.

And now, with a click of our heels (they're prettier than a gavel) and a sip of our Earl Grey (or some Moët & Chandon, it's in my pretty cabinet), let's get to work!

══ NOTEBOOK TIME: YOUR TO-DO'S ══

Wherever I go, my glittery notebook—a beautiful one that speaks to my heart—is either in my hand or resting in my purse. This carefully selected notebook holds my hopes, dreams, and wishes. No one is allowed to read this book; a bold *Thou Shalt Not Read* is written on the front cover.

To begin our journey together, I would like you, too, to find a special notebook that grabs your attention. It could be sparkly or have a special saying on the front. Perhaps a beautiful waterfall adorns the cover? An inspiring quote inscribed in bold letters?

Your notebook is going to track your progress.

For now, I want you to discover a notebook that is distinctly *you*. Once discovered, hold on to it. Throughout our time together, you will fill it up with your hopes, dreams, and wishes.

Perhaps even add a shimmering Swarovski pen to your notebook.

Keep your "Uniquely Me" notebook with you at all times; you never know when inspiration will hit. As you go through this book, you will use your notebook to complete the "To-Do's" in each chapter.

= 2 =

THE PARADOX OF DECLINING FEMALE HAPPINESS

"BUT YOU DON'T understand. I don't have the time. Ever!" Her hands were gripping the stroller and there were tears of frustration in her eyes. She stared me down as I stood outside my studio, handing out complimentary class cards to passersby. In my perky manner, I had started to tell her about the benefits of pole dancing. "Oh my god, it's so much fun! You build strength in a flirty way, it's not like being part of a gym. Come try a free—"

Before I could finish my pitch, though, her arm stretched out, thrusting her hand in my face. "Stop. When I am not at work, I am chasing after the kids. And if I do have time to myself, all I want to do is sleep. I'm exhausted. Working out is not going to happen." She stormed off down the street, leaving me holding the free class card.

Granted, my "over-the-top enthusiastic" demeanour could be annoying. However, I do understand her. I've been there too.

As I have come to witness, many women find themselves juggling the demands of work, home, and family. As a mom of a toddler and a preschooler, my days were spent racing from place to place. From 2001 to 2006, my life was work to home to afterschool activities for my boys. Extended time to myself felt like a memory that was no longer in reach. When I did grab a moment, all I wanted to do was sit on the couch and soothe myself with television and snacks. My excitement at being alive had been sucked away and I felt like a robot, going through the motions of daily existence.

One night on the phone, I lamented to my father, describing the pressures of raising a family and building a career. Overwhelmed with work, daycare, and household responsibilities, I gained close to 40 pounds through stress and bingeing on food. I had resigned myself to this overweight, uncomfortable body, hidden away under layers of clothing. Any garments that felt revealing or which clung to my body were thrown away in anger. Secretly, I resented women who were fit and thin, because it seemed that life had blessed them with more time and energy.

As a preschool teacher, my energy and enthusiasm always needed to be on point; I was always performing. Every day. Every. Single. Day. To meet the workplace expectations, I would force myself to find excitement and enjoyment even though I was physically and emotionally exhausted.

I was failing.

Failing at work.

Failing at being the kind of mother I wanted to be.

And lastly, failing to feel a true sense of excitement about life.

An Immediate Need for Change

Each morning on my way to work, I imagined myself veering my car into one of the tall maple trees I passed. This vision of slamming my car into the trunk of a tree brought tears to my eyes, and I'd arrive at work with mascara smudges. I quickly wiped them away so no one would know I was struggling. I didn't want to expose my unhappy face. Deep down, I realized my suicidal ideation was a scream for help and a call for immediate change. I couldn't go on any further, and instead of taking one extreme measure, I chose another.

"I have to quit... I am so unhappy," I whispered to the centre supervisor, Stephanie. Ah, what sweet relief to say those words out loud. As soon as they were out, I felt it.

Stephanie looked at me and shook her head. "Umm... What do you mean you're quitting?"

I responded, equally surprised as the words tumbled out of my mouth, "I know. I can't believe I'm saying it. I feel this is the only way out. I just can't keep doing this any longer."

With my supervisor's help, we hatched a plan for the bold move: leaving my career in order to maintain my sanity. The exhaustion of fighting my impulses was wearing me down, and I feared that one day the "Maple Tree Slam Plan" would actually happen. We decided I would give three months' notice for my position.

Now all I had to do was break the news to my husband. Note to self: when you make a major life-changing decision, if you are in a committed relationship, you may want to have the "I'm quitting my career" chat before you actually do it.

That evening at dinner, while passing the big bowl of spaghetti, I broke the news to Michael.

"Oh! Guess what?! I quit my job today."

He froze with the bowl in his hand. "What do you mean you quit?"

Allow me to say, that spaghetti dinner will go down in history as one of the longest Wednesday meals we have ever had! As our barely touched noodles grew cold, we debated the ramifications of my decision. Michael was an entrepreneur, and up until that day I had been an employee with full benefits, a salary, and a paid vacation. Mine was the safety net income for the family—the financial glue that held us together. It was not part of the plan for us to become a single-income family. As I confessed my hopelessness, he started to understand the gravity of the situation. If we didn't make a major life pivot now, we might end up facing a major life disaster instead.

We decided to figure it out.

Turns out it was the best decision.

As my last day of work approached, we turned our house into a home daycare centre so I could be with my children and become a home daycare provider. I welcomed two young toddlers, and spent my days with fingerpaints alongside my boys and our new friends. I had cut out my commute and could raise my kids while still earning. Operating a home daycare was an option for income while I shifted focus to my health and freeing up time for myself. And where did the shift lead me?

I wound up trying something totally new—taking pole dancing lessons and, one year later, opening a pole dancing studio. Never in my wildest dreams, or during that Wednesday Night Spaghetti Confessional, did I see that coming!

Under Pressure

I look back on those years, where the overwhelm and pressure propelled me to imagine drastic measures, and I often wonder: Were my experiences particular to me, or do other women feel the same way?

When I was with women my own age (early thirties) who had children roughly the same age as my boys, Matthew and Brendan, I saw the familiar look of fatigue. I figured this was how life was supposed to be: we were all exhausted, unhappy, and going through the motions.

Well, I eventually found a definitive answer to my question. Ten years later, while doing research for a speech on feeling vibrant, I stumbled upon a 2009 study by the National Bureau of Economic Research that confirmed I was NOT the only one. In fact, my discontent with my life was felt by many women.

Introducing—drum roll please, and in neon lights—the Paradox of Declining Female Happiness.

What's this paradox, you ask?

Allow me to geek out over this study!

The Paradox of Declining Female Happiness compares women of our generation with women of previous generations. The results show that although women today have more opportunities with respect to finances, education, and employment than our generational counterparts, we are stuck in overwhelm, and it is showing in our well-being. Women's unhappiness is rising—due to the extra pressures of combining home and work—and this decline is most noticeable among women in their peak child-rearing years or with young children at home.

Let's dive in a bit more, shall we?

When I found this study, it was my eureka moment. Although it felt as though I was the only one, my feelings were not peculiar to me. Many women in these child-rearing years and juggling careers were cracking under the pressure. While it is true that there are more expectations placed on us, as income earners and mothers, do we want to have these opportunities removed simply so that we can deal with things better?

After I found this study, I was chatting with a group of students from my studio. (Yes, by this point I was well into my career as a pole dance instructor.) The students were in their late twenties and early thirties. Discussing the results of the study,

I questioned, "If you had the choice, would you want to return to the expectations of women in the '60s and '70s—prior to the women's movement? Would you want to go back to that time?"

Each one of them responded with a "Hell no!" And I wholeheartedly agree.

I am grateful for the increased opportunities that women of my generation enjoy: more money, better education, and a wider range of employment opportunities. Yes, it's awesome—the world is our oyster. Our great-grandmothers, grandmothers, and mothers fought for this—and we are now reaping the rewards.

But we need to handle it better. We need to acknowledge that our lives are more complex than in the past, and honour the fact that we have opportunities and choices. Now, let's use this knowledge to gain confidence, strength, and inspiration. We can better handle the expectations placed on us by making clearer decisions and choices. We need healthy strategies for handling "life's overwhelm" and taking care of our well-being, so that we can enjoy our increased opportunities in finances, education, and employment. This is a much better approach than drastic solutions.

In fact, I am beginning to see this happen.

The other day, while standing in line at Starbucks to order my grande caramel coconut milk latte with no whip (my coffee orders are extra), I overheard two moms sitting at the table beside me. With their babies fast asleep in their strollers, the mamas were enjoying their handcrafted Frappuccinos. One mama was sharing her decision to schedule time for herself—where she could chill out, exercise, or do whatever she wanted to do. It was her scheduled "me time" and she was firm on that.

"It's on the calendar—written with a big bold Sharpie marker!"

I laughed out loud, signalling my act of eavesdropping. Busted.

"No, no... I'm so sorry. I think it's awesome that you are dedicating time for yourself. It took me years and near disaster to make that decision," I explained.

The mama continued to share. "I'm at peace with not getting everything done in a day. No more pressure of perfection."

To me, that is a true "I got this" moment.

NOTEBOOK TIME: YOUR TO-DO'S

Time to roll up your sleeves and seriously look at the expectations you have placed on yourself.

Make a list of your expectations. (Don't worry, I'm with you on this.) Take a look at every aspect of your life—personal, professional, how you act with your family and friends.

Whatever expectations pop into your head, write them down, creating a total brain dump of "I expect..."

- The ones that are bringing you joy, happiness, and success—give them a beautiful, shiny gold star!

- The ones that are making you miserable, teary, and depressed—grab your pen and strike them out.

- "I expect myself to pay my bills." Yes. Slap a gold star for adulting.

- "I expect myself to make everyone like me." Big red strike-through for that one, please.

- "I expect to have time set aside for myself to chill and do what I want." Shine that one up.

- "I expect to answer every request placed upon me, as quickly as possible." Slash and burn it down.

Time to bust that paradox and toss those misery-inducing expectations aside. Instead of bringing you joy and success, they are dragging you down and making your life unhappy. The decisions you make for yourself in one season of your life may no longer be appropriate in the next. Imagine the freedom of dropping the emotional weight. Look out, you are going to fly!

— 3 —

THE
UP TO
NO GOOD
CLUB

T WAS 1984. As the school bell rang, I jumped from my chair, grabbing my fourth-grade family history assignment and stuffing it in my bag. The task was to interview a parent or grandparent about their childhood—where they lived, did they have a TV, did they have a phone. All those questions a kid in the '80s would have about the past. I knew I could knock out that assignment quickly and then head to tap dance class that night. I would just interview my mom and then off I'd go with a "tap step ball change." Jazz hands and all!

Meandering down the park path, as my house came into view, I noticed my dad's car parked in the driveway. He was home two hours earlier than usual. Being an engineer, he enjoyed structure and routine. Like clockwork, he was always home by 5:40 p.m. From the park path, as I stared at his car, a sinking feeling crept in.

Mom was sick again.

Dad never arrived early from work unless it was an emergency, and the emergency was always around my mom's illness.

Manic depression was the cause of my mother's suffering. At that time, in the 1980s, the shame around mental illness was intense. Our neighbours were aware, because my mom would tell them about her struggles—to which my father would react by begging, "Please stop telling the neighbours." However, sharing her difficulties helped her feel connected, and she wanted to feel better.

As the front door swung open, my father guided Mom towards the car, one arm protectively wrapped around her shoulders while the other carried a small paper bag of pills. Mom's hair was dishevelled, her eyes were red and swollen, and her feet gingerly stepped forward to secure her footing as she walked. She clung tightly to my father for guidance and steadiness.

As she walked, I could tell that Mom was experiencing the world as hazy and out of focus. By eight years of age, I had seen these mannerisms, and they always resulted in an extended visit to the hospital. After she ingested too many medications at once, it was only a matter of time before loss of consciousness would take hold and Dad was racing against the clock to get her to the hospital. If she passed out at home, a scene involving an ambulance, sirens, and flashing lights would be the talk of the neighbourhood.

As my father opened the passenger door, my mother froze. She had noticed my presence on the path. The corners of her mouth weakly curled upwards, as her squinting eyes met mine. Her shoulders lowered and she hung her head in defeat. My eyes started to burn as I instantly felt her shame.

Slam!

Between the park path and our driveway, our neighbour's front door swung open and shut as Mrs. Carter stepped onto her porch, a tray in her hand. She was a petite woman in her sixties who loved gospel music and Sunday morning evangelist TV shows. Getting ready to enjoy her afternoon teatime, she surveyed the scene—my father guiding my mom into the car and me wiping my tears. Instantly, she knew something was wrong and placed her tea set on the table.

"Janie, come on over to my porch. Let's have a cup of tea and cookies and you can tell me about school."

Exhale. Thank heavens for Mrs. Carter's oatmeal chocolate chip cookies and a sunny porch to stay on until my brother got home from school.

As my father closed the passenger door, he called out to Mrs. Carter, "Thank you so much. I'll be at the hospital for a while to get Cheryll settled, but Jane's grandmother is on her way to stay with us."

My heart started to feel better. My grandmother was coming! Everything was going to be okay. While I sat on Mrs. Carter's porch, sipping afternoon tea and nibbling on delicious freshly baked creations, she sat down beside me.

"Janie, I'm going to let you in on a little secret. When times get tough, folks will stick together. We always help each other out. *Cheering people on is what we do best.*"

I took those words to heart.

A Different Childhood

Throughout my childhood, this was a familiar scene. My mom's depression and schizophrenia would overwhelm our household. Being a child of a parent who suffered horribly from mental illness, I had a different childhood from my friends whose mothers were healthy and present. Many times each year, my mother had hospital stays, to stabilize after a crisis. At home, her mental state would falter; she would hear voices and laugh along with them. A neighbour's house would become my haven of respite and support. I found sanctuary outside my home.

I learned to sew my dance costumes from Mrs. Jones. I learned to cook and bake from Mrs. Devenne. When I got my first period, my friend Heather's mom talked to me about sanitary products and how to handle cramps.

I came to understand that my mother tried her best. She didn't want to suffer from the darkness she faced. With the support of multiple psychiatrists, she began to feel better, experiencing periods of stability—fully awake during the day, completing projects, following her own daily routine. Then she would spiral, suffering from crying spells as she hid in her bedroom for weeks, staying awake all night and sleeping through the day. By my 13th birthday, I realized that coping with Mom's ups and downs was a part of our family life, and our mother–daughter connection would be different from what my peers experienced and enjoyed with their moms.

Part of a Community

After the birth of my first child when I was in my late twenties, it was my church community and my mother-in-law who came over to make me a cup of tea and helped out around the home. Over the first six weeks, weekly drop-offs of tuna noodle casseroles fuelled our sleep-deprived new-parent journey, and I was left with a valuable observation that has carried me through my life.

Mrs. Carter was right.

People help each other.

We encourage each other to improve, grow, and succeed in life.

When we band together, the collective energy wave pulls us together and great change is possible.

We share our tears and we share our laughter. When one of us falls, we reach down to lift them up. Being part of a community can provide the support to move your life forward—to live a rich and vibrant existence. Through social connections, we add new elements and insights by learning from each other. Community opens our world and encourages us to start trying new ideas and approaches to life; we become inspired by other people's experiences. Encouragement and support fuel us through the tough times. Community is the most powerful group I have ever experienced.

"Up Your Ziggy with a Wawa Brush"

And so, allow me to share with you . . . the Up To No Good Club and how community helped out a dear friend.

Layla Duvay was a high school teacher during the day and an enthusiastic pole student in the evenings. Starting pole dance classes in her early fifties, she devoured everything pole-related. Even though she lived in Ontario and practised at the studios in her area, she would drive to pole jams in the American Midwest just to meet more pole students. Talk about commitment to the craft and dedication to the connections! Her pole obsession brought her great joy. (FYI: pole jams are like meet-ups of pole students, who rent space in a studio to play and teach each other moves.)

Flipping her blond hair, embracing her Mae West voluptuous body, and wearing these badass Goth boots, she was like a lioness as she crawled around her pole. By posting her practice videos on Facebook, she connected with other lovers of pole, creating a network of people who could cheer each other on with a "You're fuckin' awesome!"

She was loud.

She was bold.

She was brash and loved to exclaim "Pucker up!" while showing off her booty shorts with big red lipstick kisses and telling her friends on Facebook, "I'm drinking deeply from the fountain of youth called Dance!"

One morning, while she was performing a chair spin on the pole, her hand inadvertently released its grip and she crashed to the floor. Chalking it up to overtiredness, she decided to rest and play on the poles another day. However, the tingling in her arm continued, and by the end of the week the sensation had progressed into relentless headaches. One side of her body seemed to have a delayed response as she walked or reached for objects. Shrugging it off, she mentioned her symptoms to her doctor, who took the matter seriously and ordered tests.

In her brain, a glioblastoma had formed, rooting itself into her tissue with a solid grasp. Life expectancy would be up to 18 months.

Upon learning her diagnosis, she tearfully confessed to me, "Life expires, I know this. I just don't want to fade away as the end comes near. I don't want to be forgotten."

To ease her fears, three members from the pole community—Patricia, Dani-Lee, and I—created a special group. Although we belonged to separate studios, we developed a friendship through our love for Layla, creating the "Up To No Good" Girls—our weekly version of "Coffee Klatch Throwback." The term "coffee klatch" comes from the German word *kaffeeklatsch*, which means coffee (*kaffee*) and gossip (*klatsch*). Coffee klatches were popular from the 1950s through to the 1980s. Neighbours would get together, gathering around the coffee cake with a cup of Taster's Choice to discuss the latest updates in their (and other people's) lives. Being lovers of all things vintage, we decided to bring back the klatch! I was a long way from Mrs. Carter's porch, but the idea was the same: people reinforcing each other.

Our "Up To No Good" version of a regular coffee group involved watching chick flicks, gossiping, painting Layla's nails, and marvelling at the personal pole dancing videos created in her honour by her fellow pole enthusiasts throughout North America. When asked, "What are your plans this afternoon?" our response was, "Oh, we are up to no good!"

To remind Layla that she was queen, we created a crown full of rhinestones and decorated her room with feathered boas.

Our motto was "Up Your Ziggy with a Wawa Brush." It came from the movie *The Hairy Bird* (also known as *All I Wanna Do*) in the scene where Gaby Hoffmann tells off Kirsten Dunst for being too nosy. Once we heard it, causing us to nearly pee our pants with laughter, it became our secret club cheer. (To this day, when someone annoys me, I quietly whisper to myself, "Up your ziggy.")

Live Big, Dream Big, and Love Big

Through the slow decline of Layla's health and body, we made sure she was loved and cared for—not forgotten and left out. When her spirits were down, our twerking contest would give her a lift. We'd line up in front of her so she could judge who bounced their booty the best. (I never won. My booty can't twerk.) With our hair tossing, body waving, and booty shaking galore, our gang helped Layla pass to the other side, honouring her fierce and courageous spirit along her journey.

Gathering in Layla's high school classroom to honour her rebellious spirit during her Celebration of Life, Dani-Lee, Patricia, and I reminisced about how she had taught us to live big, dream big, and love big. As hard as it is to lose a dear friend and unique individual, we recognized how our lives were better because of her. We pledged to never turn down the volume on our uniqueness. Giggling at the mischief we experienced in the 18 months of life that remained to her after her diagnosis, we saluted this lioness who never faded as she rocked on to the other side.

Community is all around us, with folks ready to lift each other up. As you embark on this journey of reinvention, extend a hand and gather people around you who want to keep your shiny crown in place, the way we did for Layla. Also, be sure to give back and look for people to applaud.

══ NOTEBOOK TIME: YOUR TO-DO'S ══

1 **Create your own Up To No Good Club.**
Although being up to no good with friends is a blast, let's be honest, it can be tricky. When we were teens, hanging out with friends outweighed sleep and homework. Now that we're grown-ups, for most of us the situation is reversed: sleep and work create a challenge for maintaining friendships. Our social circle shrinks. Work responsibilities and life commitments pile up sky-high, and many of us are living the "work and hide" rhythm. And, as of early 2020, let's throw in a global pandemic to make it even harder to create community.

Grab your notebook and add the goal of making connections, busting the barrier of solitude, and opening your world. Add some stars and hearts if you like.

Where do you start?

Begin with your current friend group. Reach out to the people whose energy you have enjoyed and whom you have cheered on in their lives. So often, we drop out of each other's lives simply because we are busy. Choose to drop back in with a "Hello! Life's been busy and I've missed you" message to get the reconnection ball rolling again, with the intent to strengthen the friendship bond.

If you are feeling you need a rest from your current social circle, why not bring some new connections into your life? Look for communities built on similar interests. They are all around us. Meetup is an excellent resource. In my area, a Meetup search pulls up:

- Always Hiking!
- Westend Lesbians
- FTDTW (Friends To Do Things With)
- I Talk To Strangers And Make Friends
- Coffee Meet Up
- Social Dance Party
- Dungeons And Dragons 4ever
- LGBTQ & Meditation
- Happy Hour Zoom Call for QTBIPOC

And those are just in my area. Imagine what's in yours. Sign up and give it a shot!

If joining Meetup makes you feel uncomfortable (or if it's not possible due to lockdown), think about joining an online Facebook community. Turn to your Facebook and click on Groups. The "Suggested for You" feature will appear and, yes, it's creepy how much Facebook knows about us. That being said, use it to your advantage and see what groups are available for you to join. Allow the algorithms to help you meet people.

2 **Create an "I'm a Rock Star" evidence file on your computer (or in your "Uniquely Me" notebook).**
Let's look at how you are filling yourself up. Are you motivating yourself or dragging yourself down?

Your voice is the most important one in your life. When filled with positivity and grace, it will lead you to your hopes and dreams. The power in the words you speak to yourself is incredible, so ensure your voice is positive. You're deserving of kind, loving words and a wealth of inner strength and encouragement.

In a file folder on your computer or in your notebook, gather proof of your awesomeness: emails from people singing your praises, photos and images of your winning moments. By documenting your awesomeness, you create a system of celebrating your wins.

I love keeping track of my little wins. Throughout the week, I look for moments where life seems to be going my way. Doesn't matter the size of the win, because small wins add up. Got a free coffee? That's a win. Only had green lights while driving to work? That's a win. Someone complimented you? Write that down. Save it because, when you hit a bump, your evidence file will remind you of your greatness.

Look, we are all figuring it out as we go along. Doing it by ourselves, trying to make our way in the world without the support of others, can be freaking lonely. Surround yourself with people who embrace your imperfections and encourage your dreams. Your journey will be filled with love and glitter confetti.

4

THE POLARIZATION OF SEXINESS

THE OUTDOOR HEALTH and Wellness Festival on Kerr Street in Oakville was slowly filling up with spectators throughout the sunny June morning. After setting up the pole stage in my booth, I spun around the pole to gather attention and promote my new studio. Pole demonstrations at trade shows and events were a big part of my business launch plan, and I couldn't wait to get started, showing the world my moves. I'd keep going for as long as my body could stand it.

My studio was only a week old, and the trade show was my entrance into the world as a business owner. It was also an opportunity to display my passion for pole dancing. This was business owner "go time," and I was all decked out in my freshly screen-printed, logoed red tank top and new Lululemon skort (think tennis skirt/short with a ruffly bottom). Look out, world!

As I flipped upside down on the pole, climbed, and demonstrated holds, a crowd would gather in front of me. Once I'd attracted a captive audience, I would hand out my business cards, encouraging them to check out my new studio and sign up for a class. "Come to our Grand Opening!"

The morning was fantastic. The pole and I were a big hit. Until, that is, a voice pierced through the crowd:

"You! You are a vulgar woman!"

I froze. Upside down on the pole. Not an easy feat, I might add. Instantly, I knew the voice was directed at me.

The shriek belonged to a short woman in her fifties, and she was *glaring*. As I descended the pole, I instantly knew who had yelled at me because people were looking at her—then at me—waiting for a showdown between the girl on the pole and her accuser. Grab your popcorn, it looks like a fight is on!

I approached her and said, "No, no, I'm not doing anything wrong! I'm opening a studio and I want to help people feel sexy and strong."

She snapped back, "It's vulgar. Look at you. Look how you are dressed. Vulgar."

I was wearing typical workout clothing. My skort covered my cheeks; my gluteal fold was concealed from the world. (What's a gluteal fold, you ask? It's where the top of your thigh and lower section of your buttocks connects.)

"And this—whatever you are disguising it as—it belongs… you know, in those places."

Oh, hello, stigma. You're back! The phrase "those places" tended to be a snide reference to strip clubs.

"A respectable woman would never do this," she barked out as her last jab before storming off.

As the crowd stood fixed in place, staring at me frozen at my pole, I could feel my heart begin to pound. I was both angry at her and embarrassed at my naïveté about other people's viewpoint on pole dancing. Here I was, face to face with judgment in front of a crowd. Within one hour of proclaiming to the world my love of pole dancing, I was met with wrath and judgment. I stepped off my portable pole stage and covered up my tank top with my hoodie.

I shelved my plans to demonstrate pole moves, opting to hand out my free class cards instead. Decision made, I had four hours left at the festival. *I'll just kill time,* I told myself, *quickly pack up the pole, and run back home.*

During the first hour, I stayed away from my booth, hanging out instead at the Free Smoothie Samples booth (my tradeshow-marketing husband would cringe to read this). On my return from the umpteenth free smoothie run, I found a woman staring at my booth, marvelling at the shiny pole stage. In the stroller beside her was a sleeping toddler. Her eyes caught mine and she instantly smiled. "Oh! I've been hearing all about this! Could you do some moves for me?"

I zipped up my hoodie and took a sip of my smoothie. "I'm sorry, I'm on a break, but you can come take a class for free."

As I pulled out the card from my hoodie pocket, she smiled. "This is exactly what I need. This year has been all about baby, and I feel so gross inside. I don't feel... you know... sexy. Just covered in baby spit-up and poop all the time. Thanks for the card—I'll definitely check your website out. I really wish I had come earlier to see you do your moves. That would have been cool."

As she spoke, she reminded me of myself when I was starting out. I too began classes because I was in the grips of motherhood and needed something—anything—that wasn't toddler-like! This lady was exactly me two years earlier. Inside, the pit of shame from my prior "vulgar encounter" dissolved as a renewed inner push to succeed emerged.

She started to push her stroller away, heading towards the smoothie booth.

"Wait! I can show you a pole hold!"

"Oh my god, really?! What's that?"

I walked up to the stage and wrapped my hands around the shiny pole. Using my biceps and shoulders, I lifted myself up, pointing my toes and flipping my hair back.

She squealed. "I love it! That's hot! Do you have any classes tomorrow? Count me in."

That was the moment I realized that not everyone was going to like my work. I thought, *I am going to be judged and ridiculed. However, there will be people who find inspiration and are willing to join in.* I would have to put myself out there, talk about feeling sexy and strong in life, and weed through the shamers. The ones who no longer wanted to play it safe and were eager to move out of their comfort zone would be discovered.

Sexiness can be polarizing.

The Idea of Sexy

As I learned from my experience at the Health and Wellness Festival, people have strong reactions to the idea of sexiness and feeling sexy. Talking about sexiness can make people feel uncomfortable. Many times, when I bring up the subject of feeling sexy or sexiness, the receiver will either lean in or pull away, eager to change the subject or completely shut it down with, "Yeah. No. I don't do sexy."

Often, when I receive a call from someone who wants to sign up for classes, I'll hear, "I'm just taking the class for fitness. I don't want to do that sexy stuff." Just between us, within weeks of taking their first pole class, it is guaranteed that person will start moving towards the sexy side of pole and ask where to find those clear Lucite heels. I love it when that happens!

Sharing ideas around sexiness is my jam. A playfulness takes over when I talk about feeling sexy in our lives. I know we are breaking rules when we delve into this topic. To be honest with you, as an '80s baby, I don't recall having a high comfort level when talking about feeling sexy in my pre-pole life. It was a hidden subject . . . and still is! Now, I get a zap of energy and a mischievous smile on my face when I'm with a group and we start to openly share stories.

Reactions to the word "sexy" fascinate me. Some are defensive and angry (remember the "vulgar" accusation?) while others are curious and playful. I try not to judge the strong responses because at one point in my life I felt repulsed by the idea too.

In my pre–pole dancing life, I felt uncomfortable in my body—bloated, sluggish, and tired. (When you're a mom, your diet of the kids' leftover mac 'n' cheese and chicken fingers can sometimes leave you feeling . . . ugh.) Did I feel sexy during this time? Not a chance. I hated sexiness and would react in anger whenever my husband uttered the word "lingerie." On top of this, if I saw a woman who looked sexy and confident in her body—I instantly hated her. How dare she!

Keeping my own early reaction to "sexiness" in mind, I started asking my students how they felt about this topic. Jennifer, 34 years old, married with two children, shared with me that "sexy" was not how she wanted to describe herself, because she worked as a teacher. (I'm trying very hard to refrain from "sexy teacher" analogies!) Her job was one wrapped in responsibilities and role-modelling. It had become her identity. She was responsible and hard-working, while "sexy" was a feeling she associated with being young and carefree. Those were two adjectives that she felt no longer applied to her.

For many women, their preconceived ideas of sexiness got in the way—whether it was messages they received from family or experiences with friends. Sarah shared that her family's views on how women should act played a major role in how she behaved. "Dressing modest and being sensible in my appearance was taught from a young age. When I was nine years old, I borrowed my friend's tank top and got in trouble with my grandmother for baring my shoulders. I was discouraged from showing skin, so as an adult I felt uncomfortable wearing clothing that showed my body."

Vanessa, aged 28, remembered when she was 10 years old and hanging out with her friends. A woman walked by dressed in a short skirt and heels. One friend quickly snickered, "Oh my god, what a slut," and instantly Vanessa realized she never wanted anyone to think of her that way. As an adult, if a woman dressed in form-fitting clothing walked by her, the memory would flash into her mind and she would have to fight the impulse to judge. She intentionally chose clothing that prevented her from being *that* woman. Mindfulness helped her reframe her trigger to mentally slut-shame.

Moving Away from Judgment

How did these women go from feeling angry, judgmental, and shamed to feeling comfortable in their own skin, viewing themselves as beautiful and sexy creatures? For many of them, it was a result of nurturing their bodies and healing their self-image. They came to recognize that their self-image had been kicked around by life experiences, such as divorce and betrayal, and they took the time to care for the ego bruise with love, kindness, and grace. Like wounded birds, these women built nests around themselves in order to give themselves the space to heal. These women identified that they were worthy of love and nurturing—that ultimately, it was up to them to rebuild. They allowed themselves to face their perceptions, tackle the issues from the past, and create a revival.

Jennifer, the teacher whose identity was saturated with responsibility, realized that being care*free* didn't make her care*less*. She could let loose and it wouldn't lead her to be irresponsible. But her fear of getting in trouble always held her back, so she and her husband planned a trip to an Adults Only resort (yes, THAT kind of resort!). By creating this secret getaway, she gave herself an opportunity to have fun and break rules in a safe environment. She reconnected with her partner because she felt free. She felt joy in breaking the rules she had set for herself.

Sarah, whose family encouraged her to never show skin, went to a burlesque show. She witnessed people embracing their curves, adorning their bodies with Swarovski crystals and glitter. It was a world she had never witnessed, and she was mesmerized by these performers who unapologetically showed off their bodies. "I was expecting to see the stereotypical skinny performer—you know, the ones with the perfect body. Instead, I saw regular bodies. Curves, rolls, skin, dimples, cellulite—different shapes and sizes. And they didn't hide—quite the opposite, they showed off their body differences. They made their rolls shake. It was the purest form of body acceptance I have ever seen."

As a burlesque performer myself, I can attest to this form of body love and acceptance. From 2010 to 2016, I performed as Ms. Natalia Rose in shows throughout Toronto and St. Louis, as a pole performer. I witnessed a celebration of body diversity like no other. Being naked in front of 500 people may seem intimidating, but when you experience it, while covered in sparkle and an attitude of "I'm a motherfuckin' goddess," you step off the stage with a take-no-prisoners confidence. My time in the burlesque community taught me to be a better performer (onstage and off) and also that the conventions of perceived perfectionism don't apply. This is a culture where everyone is beautiful and celebrated. We are all beautiful naked.

Vanessa overcame her temptation to judge other women by becoming more self-aware. Once she identified that her hostility was rooted in her childhood, she worked hard to rewire her brain. In fact, she purposefully took exotic dance classes to force herself to face her judgments. Soon, she stopped making internal comments during her classes. She knew she had made a breakthrough when she was in a store and tried on a short skirt... and didn't feel any shame. And yes, she bought the skirt—and many more items of form-fitting clothing!

Sometimes, we may be only beginning to learn what sexiness means to us. Rav, 26 years old, recently completed her university degree and has begun working full-time. Up until now, her life has been a mix of schoolwork, friends, and growing up. Living in a female-dominated household—it's a house of three women and her father ("we make him do the dishes")—her upbringing was geared towards education and becoming a strong, outspoken, and confident woman. The notion of feeling sexy in life never came up, and she wonders if it's a discussion she could have with her sisters. At this moment, she is beginning to explore her own definition of sexiness, which, up until now, was mostly derived from the media, TV, and movies—all of which showed people projecting sexiness through their clothing and body styles. For herself, she's defining sexiness as a feeling that comes from within. Some days she feels sexy and others she does not, the same way that some days she is happy and others she is not. It's all a question of life's ups and downs.

A state of being. She could be covered in dirt from working on her farm and still feel sexy.

Julie Brand of Studioveena agrees. In 2008, Julie created Studioveena.com, an online community that anyone can join to learn to pole dance at home. She has since taught over 20,000 people throughout the world. She feels sexiness is a part of our emotional health—another aspect of our feelings. It's part of the balance of who we are as people. "I think, as women, we don't focus on it enough. We focus on our diet, getting in shape. When we are focusing on feeling sexy and loving our bodies for how they are right now, then everything falls into place." Then we treat our bodies with more love and kindness.

When she was younger, Julie viewed being sexy as a bad thing—wrong and dirty. It was forbidden. She felt guilty for wanting to feel sexy, and never saw herself as attractive. Right before she turned 30, she decided to allow herself to open up to feeling sexy. She found a partner who was not judgmental and encouraged her to explore. She felt safe and secure in her relationship. Now, she feels at ease with herself and completely confident in her body. She can wear sexy clothing and not feel self-conscious or ashamed. By following this quest to feel at peace with her body, she has led people around the world to be kinder to themselves and more positive towards their bodies.

Kelly Lee, 57, broke some rules when she started dating younger men. Divorced at age 47, she decided, as a newly single woman, to date within her own age group. Then she allowed herself to be open to change. "One summer, while new windows were being installed in my home, I was chatting with the builders. Next thing I realized, I had a date with a cute window installer! He was younger than me. Much younger. I thought the rule was to date your age and up. I gladly broke it."

When she asked her son what he thought, he responded with, "As long as it's legal, it's okay."

Ten years later, Kelly Lee is enjoying a fun and adventurous relationship with her partner, Bill, whom she met online and who is 22 years younger. Feeling energized and thriving in life, she dared to go against the norm, even being featured in a UK TV documentary about age differences in relationships.

Stepping out of our comfort zone and rethinking our perspective on sexiness opens up new possibilities. From new possibilities, a youthful energy appears, providing our lives with a recharge. New adventures are ahead when we allow ourselves to break free of rules and personal judgment, as though we are shedding our old skin to reveal a beautiful new surface.

═══ NOTEBOOK TIME: YOUR TO-DO'S ═══

Let's dip a toe by answering the following prompt:

I feel sexy when…

One afternoon in our Up To No Good Club Facebook group—a special group for those who want to feel strong, sexy, and confident—I posed the question, "When do you feel sexy?"

The answers flooded in!

What surprised me were the non-pole-related answers—how they were feeling outside the studio, as they lived their lives.

- "I have an enthusiasm for life. Then it doesn't matter what you are wearing." AMY

- "I feel sexier in high heels and a cool outfit. AND in my Lululemon pants. Man, my ass looks amazing in them!" ANDREA

- "I carve out time for myself, to foster my own identity and explore my own ideas." JEN

- "I always feel sexy after a long hot bubble bath." JULIE

- "Strong. Either physically or mentally." CHRISTINE

- "When I am being 100% myself. Unapologetically quirky." KAREN

- "When I am uninhibited and authentic. Being present and embracing myself." ALEXANDRIA

- "When I feel free and open to new experiences." JOANNA

- "I know I am doing very well if I have time to shave my legs and moisturize! That's good enough for me to feel sexy. With everything going on in my life—between kids, husband, and career—if I get my legs shaven, then I am winning!" STEPHANIE

Now it's your turn. Remember, there's no right or wrong to how you feel. You can add a lot of responses or just a few. Use your answers to inspire and ignite your sexy side.

I feel sexy when _____.

DARE
YOURSELF

N AUGUST 1982, wearing my purple Duran Duran T-shirt, I dangled my legs in the pool water, waiting with eager anticipation for the Patricia Anne Memorial Swim-A-Thon to begin. Off to the side, spectators gathered on the bleachers, with homemade signs like *You Can Do This, Cheryll!* written in blue, red, and black markers. On hand to report about the event, a journalist and photographer from our town's newspaper, the *Oakville Beaver*, joined the crowd. We were all waiting to cheer on my mother for her fundraiser, designed to raise money for two small children, aged 21 months and 9 years, who had witnessed their mother being butchered to death by her boyfriend. Leaving the children in the care of their uncle, who was finding it hard to carry the extra financial burden, the murder had shocked the 75,000 residents of suburban Oakville, especially my mother. Although she had never met Patricia Anne, she identified deeply with the tragedy.

The early signs of my mother's mental health struggles were starting to appear, and the horrific tragedy shattered her morale. Patricia's older daughter was the same age as me. At a young age, my mother lost her own mother to a nervous breakdown; she was committed, and remained institutionalized for the rest of her life. The thought of Patricia's daughters continuing their lives, motherless, set off her unresolved grief. The "depression beast" was raising its head, prompting a dark beginning to the summer.

The official sunny season kickoff began with the opening of the neighbourhood public pool. Located in the park near our home, Lawson Pool was the hangout for us kids. We'd wait anxiously with our faces pressed against the wire fence, counting down to the opening of the gates and the first splash of the season. The community pool was our babysitter, as our moms enjoyed their afternoon peace and quiet. "Get out! Go to the pool!" could be heard after lunch in every house, and we'd dash to the pool, wearing our bathing suits. We lived in those suits. By the late afternoon, the pool also became the hangout for the moms—wearing their one-piece, ruffled suits along with matching bathing caps to keep their hair dry. They gathered, gossiped, and shared their housekeeping ideas. On the periphery of the watery circle of gab, my mother floated on the surface, allowing the weightlessness to melt away her tension.

In the pool, my mother had always found tranquility.

As the neighbourhood moms blabbed about the recent murder, my mom could feel the tension rise. Feelings of frustration and helplessness would take over as she listened to the gabbing.

"I heard the uncle can't afford to care for the girls," Mrs. Lewis announced to the group. "He doesn't have enough money, and there was no insurance left behind."

Jolted by the gossip, my mom dove over to the group. "Will they take the girls away from their family?" she questioned.

"Well, if he can't afford to care for them . . . who knows?" Mrs. Lewis shrugged.

My mother's body started to shake, the gravity of the situation unfolding in her mind.

"There's gotta be something we can do. We HAVE to do something for those little girls," my mother pleaded.

The ladies shrugged and turned away from her to gossip about the latest episode of *The Young and the Restless*, leaving my mother treading water, grasping for solutions.

That night, over ham and scalloped potatoes, my mother shared her anguish with my father. What could she do to help? She was a stay-at-home mom, struggling with her inner demons. Every day was a fight for energy. How would she push through helplessness to make a difference? She needed to do something. She could knit, sew, and weave. Sell her wares to raise money for the girls? That would take a long time, and their family desperately needed immediate assistance.

What else could she do?

"I can swim," she realized.

Swimming brought her freedom; the watery refuge calmed her nerves. Gliding through the water, feeling the coolness envelop her body as it propelled forward, cutting through the surface, brought her a feeling of serenity. She could swim laps from one end of the pool to the other and back without a rest or touching the ground, to raise money for the motherless daughters. This 35-year-old mother of two who fought every day for her sanity was going to use her coping mechanism to contribute to two young children's well-being.

For two weeks, she canvassed the community, telling her neighbours, "I'll swim until my arms fall off" to raise money.

"Please support me to do this. Whatever you can give for these children," she would tell our neighbours. Dollar by dollar, funds for the Swim-A-Thon grew, with one man calling to pledge $20 for every 15 minutes of continuous lengths without stopping.

The big newspapers, the *Toronto Sun* and *Toronto Star*, caught wind of the Swim-A-Thon. With the headline "Strokes for Little Folks," they discussed the murder and boosted the appeal for funds. The article quoted my mother: "I may not be an attractive swimmer, but we need more charity and less tragedy in our world." Her gesture struck a public nerve. Funds rolled in in bucketsful.

Before a crowd of well-wishers, reporters, and photographers, she stood at the top of the pool wearing her one-piece red bathing suit. Cheryll Konzuk, a sufferer of manic depression, rose out of her struggles and raised $2,100 (equivalent to $5,400 today). Before diving into the water and swimming non-stop for three hours, she met my eyes and I discovered, *Wow, my mother is strong.*

Decades later, when Mom passed away from a stroke in 2013, as I cleaned out her top dresser drawer, I found an old, weathered scrapbook. Opening the cover, I discovered old newspaper articles pasted to the yellowed pages. Instantly, I recognized the first article from the *Oakville Beaver* about the Swim-A-Thon. Mom clipped all the articles, and gathered up the well-wishing cards, posters, and notes, to create a time capsule of her fortitude—a reminder of her triumph in making it to the finish line.

With a dash of bravery, action will occur. A kick in our pants, also known as daring ourselves, will create a wave of momentum, leaving us feeling braver, stronger, and armed with self-reliance. Great things happen when we push ourselves out of our comfort zone. Challenging ourselves is a way to create momentum and build up our courage muscles, so we feel stronger and more capable of facing adversity.

Be Your Own Superhero

Take one of my students, Rebecca, as an example. She was terrified of motorcycles, but intrigued by them at the same time. The vroom of the bike made her stomach feel both queasy and excited. Her daughter dragged her to motorcycle riding lessons and she joined in as a moral support. However, Rebecca failed her course exam—she turned the bike too quickly, past the point of balance, and tipped into the bushes—bruising her body and ego at the same time.

Failing the exam nagged her like a piece of unfinished business that followed her wherever she went. Deep in her heart, she knew she had to try again, to not give up and be a role model of perseverance. Initially, she had joined the course for her daughter, but now she was going to pass the exam as an act of self-redemption.

With the sun shining, she could feel the wind blow as she rode her bike on the practice course. Getting used to the weight of the bike and the intensity of the engine, Rebecca could sense her confidence increasing. With more practice, she became fierce in her ability to steer her bike.

Exam day arrived, and with a deep breath she channelled her inner Ana Carrasco[1] and passed the course with flying colours. Now she is the proud owner of a shiny red Harley-Davidson that she zooms down the street and pulls up beside

---

1 Ana Carrasco Gabarrón is a Spanish motorcycle racer who won the 2018 Supersport 300 World Championship, becoming the first woman in history to win a world championship in solo motorcycle road racing.

the studio. Flipping her hair as she takes off her helmet, she has a swagger about her because she dared to keep trying.

Psyching ourselves up to take a dare is a mental game. The "I Have Superpowers" approach comes in handy (Marvel and DC fans will love this). One of my students, Heather, relayed the story of her terrible first day at her new workplace. Being the department newbie, she felt the expected lack of certainty and fought the urge to run for the exit signs. She worried that her lack of confidence showed, that her new colleagues would doubt her ability. To combat this worry, she imagined the cartwheel pole move, which took her months to perfect. She could feel the strength in her muscles.

"I am a freakin' hero," she reminded herself, feeling her imaginary cape on her shoulders.

The idea of using your superpower—an ability that feels unique and builds up your confidence—became a hot topic one night in the Up To No Good Club Facebook group. When asked "What is your superhero power?" our students responded:

- "Right now, my ability to multi-task with extreme lack of sleep and physical discomfort. #momlife" MEGHAN

- "I'm proud of my never-ending creativity." PATRICIA

- "My lifelong hidden talent is I have a sick sense of direction. Knowing where I am and which direction to go—it's handy, helpful, and weird!" MARISSA

- "My special random talents: 1. I excel at baking cookies. 2. I pretty much know what is always divisible by four (thank you, graphic design skills). 3. I make great cocktails!" CAT

- "My makeup skills. I love playing with colours as it makes me happy. I am proud of my listening skills as it can make someone feel good to be heard." MAE

My Biggest Dare for Myself

Allow me to share with you my biggest dare as an entrepreneur. I love teaching private lessons, and it's an aspect of my business that I wanted to expand. Private lessons are great for clients who want one-on-one attention to either get better on the pole or become better performers. To expand my clientele for private lessons, I recognized that I enjoyed working with exotic dancers. With these people, we are past the "Oh my god, I don't know if I should pole dance" phase. They are already dancers and are specifically looking for pole tricks and choreography—at which I excel! I love helping them design their personality onstage and choose moves that play on their assets. And so... "Pole Tricks Lessons for Exotic Dancers" was created.

With a flyer in hand, I visited the strip clubs in my area and talked to the owners and managers about my services.

Did I tell you that many strip clubs are run by organized crime?

At the first club, I could feel the adrenalin flooding my body. I wasn't sure if it was fear of failure or fear of facing Tony Soprano that was making me vomit in my lap. I sat in my car thinking, *What the hell are you doing? This is the dumbest idea.* However, I had these beautifully designed flyers, which had cost me money, so I felt I had to use them, and I realized it was fear of failure that was keeping me from releasing the seat belt. I finally got out of the car.

With a deep breath, I opened the front door of the club and was instantly met a brawny, tall dude with RAF (also known as Resting Asshole Face, the male version of Resting Bitch Face). Wearing all black and looking as though he could bench-press 295 pounds, he sneered at me. Time to flash my great big winning smile!

"Hi there, my name is Jane Wilson. I teach pole dancing. Can I speak to the owner of this establishment, please?" I said in my most professional yet uplifting voice, accompanied by my Pollyanna grin.

He looked me up and down. "Why?" It wasn't really a question but more like a statement.

"I have an idea that will help dancers feel more confident onstage."

Rolling his eyes, he scoffed, "The owner's over there," and he pointed his stubby finger at this overweight, bald guy in a wrinkled suit.

I took a deep breath, walked up to the guy, and reached out for a handshake.

"Hi, my name is Jane Wilson and I teach pole dancing. Do your dancers feel comfortable onstage?"

"What the fuck kind of question is that?!" He was keeping his cards close to his chest.

"I mean... What I meant to say was... I help dancers feel more confident onstage. For years I have been providing private lessons for dancers, and I am looking to expand my business." I gave him a smile.

"Oh, really?" He rolled his eyes.

"Yes, really. I'm really good at it."

On the stage behind him was a tall brunette, carefully stepping around the pole as she wore dramatic seven-inch platform black leather ankle boots. By the way she gripped the pole I could tell she was careful not to roll her ankle.

"Look," I quietly pointed out to him, "see the dancer onstage—her heels are too high for her. With lessons, I can help her feel more secure."

"Yeah, but no dancer will pay for lessons or even show up." He shrugged.

And just as he finished his sentence, I felt a tap on my shoulder. Expecting it to be a bouncer ready to lead me out the door, I slowly turned around. In front of me was a tall blonde, in body wraps and fishnets. Her arms wrapped around me, giving me a welcoming hug.

"Jane? You're here!" It was Dominique, whom I had worked with for six months, helping her feel more comfortable with her inverts.

"I'm here to tell the club owner about my new private lessons program."

Dominique turned to the owner. "Harv, seriously, she helped me out. Take her info—give it to the girls. She's great."

And with that, my private lesson business exploded—all because I dared myself to walk into that club.

Life gets interesting when we dare ourselves.

I want you to feel confident and courageous.

I want you to step out of your comfort zone, to feel powerful and able to handle any obstacle that comes your way.

═══ NOTEBOOK TIME: YOUR TO-DO'S ═══

1 **Are you ready to take a dare?**
We dare ourselves in order to break routine and monotony. Time to bust out and make your list of dares. Remember, it doesn't need to be a massive dare; it can be a bite-sized mini-dare to build up your courage.

What have you always wanted to try? The moment the thought *I've always wanted to try that!* pops into your head, it's an indicator of a dare. Write it down and then put a date on it: "I want to try this by _____." Putting a date places accountability, thereby creating momentum and action.

2 **What is your superhero ninja skill?**
Make a list of skills and talents that you are proud of and keep them in the back of your mind for when you are feeling a lack of self-confidence and need to psych yourself up!

(By the way, my secret ninja skills—apart from winning pole championships: I am very computer tech savvy, and can type 70 words per minute. Thank you, grade nine typing class!)

6

WHAT'S HOLDING YOU BACK?

"OH MY GOD, now she's going on about joining this boot camp!" proclaimed the matcha latte drinker sitting beside me and having a conversation through her AirPods. "I bet she's trying to be on trend. I can't possibly see her following through on this."

Instantly, my blood boiled, as I attempted to chill out at my favourite indie roaster. As she bellowed, fellow coffee drinkers turned towards her and I realized I wasn't the only eavesdropper in the room.

"Like seriously. Let's be honest—she is not the training type of person. That's hard-core. I hope she doesn't ask me to join her."

Allow me to show you my gossipy side. Although the famous saying of Eleanor Roosevelt—"Great minds discuss ideas; average minds discuss events; small minds discuss people"—is posted on my Inspiration board, sometimes a good ole "unleash the rant" feels mighty nice as I climb up on my soapbox. Here's to *temporarily* breaking my Eleanor Roosevelt "Words to Live By" vow! Listen, Café Chick, don't sabotage your friend as she steps outside her comfort zone, simply because you are complacent in yours.

We have hopes, dreams, and ideas to explore, and we're ready to take that trust fall.[2] There we are with our arms crossed, squeezing our eyes shut and taking that deep breath—ready for the universe to catch us. Then we freeze—we start the process, easing our way backwards, and then "psych!"—we chicken out.

We worry about what our friends are going to say.

We worry about disappointing our parents.

We worry about looking like a fool.

We worry that it will involve change, effort, time, and money.

We worry about participating in an activity alone and feel safe when someone is by our side, so we wait for someone to join us, wasting time as we sit on the sidelines watching our dreams float away.

Hold on. I'm still standing on my soapbox.

My biggest pet peeve as the owner of a fitness business is hearing "I can't try this alone" when I am at an event talking to a person who seems genuinely interested in taking classes. I see the excitement at the prospect of trying something new, but then those words slide out: "I'll see if my friend will join me."

In these moments, as I bite down on my lip to stop myself from losing my mind (because THAT is not good for business), I simply smile and say, "I can't wait to see you in the studio." Deep in my heart I know it won't happen, because that friend may be going through any number of things: a divorce, the birth of a child, a new job, they've sold a house/bought a house,

---

2 A trust fall is a team-building exercise in which a participant closes their eyes and falls backwards, trusting the other team members to catch them.

they just aren't feeling well. The procrastinating excuse of "waiting for a friend" causes life to be put on pause.

I do understand. The act of starting something new, on our own, beckons us back to the first day of school. It's nerve-racking. In the book *Self-Defeating Behaviors*, contributors Mel Snyder and Arthur Frankel share how we use excuses and procrastinate on projects as a way to preserve self-esteem—to save our pride from embarrassment and failure. Excuses, as a form of procrastination, become a self-defeating behaviour, and we end up making success and achievement harder for ourselves because we are protecting our ego from failure. Our self-defeating behaviours hold us back as we seek to save ourselves from the probability of failure and disappointment.

Avoiding the "Waiting for Others" Trap

Are you waiting on someone in order to enjoy your life and chase your dream? Are you holding back on your journey as you wait for someone to make up their mind to join you? *PLEASE STOP PAUSING. GO AND DO IT!* is written in big, glittery block letters on the sign I am holding up on this imaginary soapbox.

Take my dear friend Cathryn Haynes, for example.

Cathryn had a dream of visiting Paris, to enjoy a romantic, croissant-fuelled vacation surrounded by art, fashion, wine, and culture. As a child, she imagined herself on a girls' weekend away in the City of Light—losing herself in the charm of the cobbled streets, with a bag of pastries in hand, taking pictures with her buddies in front of the Eiffel Tower. Because, you know, as Julia Ormond said in the remake of *Sabrina*, "Paris is always a good idea!"

But no one was available to go on the trip.

Cathryn's friends either were too busy, didn't have the money, or would respond with "Amazing idea, let's plan it for next year!" (Then next year would come and it would be "OMG time flies! Let's plan it for next year again!")

As time passed, Cathryn realized she was putting herself on hold, waiting for people to join in on her Paris dreams. Her wanderlust was fading, and this made her mad.

So off she went! Contacted her travel agent and *bam!* planned her first trip abroad.

Since then, she has visited:

- France (Paris)

- Italy (Rome, Venice, and Florence)

- England (London and Windsor)

- Cuba (Varadero, Havana, Cayo Santa María)

- Greece (Athens, Mykonos, Patmos, Crete, Rhodes, Santorini)

- Turkey (Istanbul and Kuşadası)

- Czech Republic (Prague and Terezín)

- Spain (Madrid, Segovia, Bilbao, San Sebastian, Pamplona, Zaragoza, Barcelona, Ibiza, Granada, Gibraltar, Seville, Córdoba, and Toledo)

- South Africa (Johannesburg, Pretoria, and Cape Town)

- New York State (New York City)

- Australia (Melbourne, Sydney, Surfers Paradise, Brisbane, Fraser Island, Baralaba, Whitsundays, Daydream Island, and Cairns)

- British Columbia (Vancouver)

- Dominican Republic (Punta Cana)

- Nevada (Las Vegas)

- Arizona (the Grand Canyon, South Rim)

- Mexico (Mayan Riviera, Cancún, Cozumel)

- Costa Rica (Tamarindo)

She's visited five continents and no longer puts her plans on hold to wait for someone to join in. Her wanderlust has led her to explore the world on her own.

Please, it's time to quit standing by as your friends decide if they want to join in your dreams. Go and do it yourself.

And now, I step down off my soapbox.

NOTEBOOK TIME: YOUR TO-DO'S

Let's revisit your list of dares. Beside the dares that you have completed, write down how you currently feel. Elation? Pride? A sense of accomplishment? By writing down your current emotion about the completed dare, you reflect on the experience and prove to yourself that you can take a risk. Fear of uncertainty is a big factor in holding ourselves back. Our brains create stories around what could happen, and procrastination creeps in as we put off the outcome.

When we look back on our accomplished dares from the other side of the experience, we prove that we survived the risk. The proof of experience builds up our courage to bust through the fears that hold us back.

In your notebook, you have validation that you can take a risk, that you have ninja skills. Your "I'm a Rock Star" file is full of evidence. Use these tools to rip away from the "holding-you-back grasp" and continue to move your life forward.

"DEAR ME, I'M SORRY"

"JANE, ARE YOU IN? I gotta know now."

The voice on the other end of my cell was full of pride at extending this invitation to the coveted North American Pole Dance Championships. For three years, I'd competed in pole championships, winning Canadian Pole Fitness Championship, Masters Division, in 2015. Receiving an invitation to this outstanding championship is a dream come true for pole competitors. As well, the stage is gorgeous, bathing the competitor in a flattering light, which guarantees excellent video you can use for promotional purposes for years to come. To win your division, competing against individuals from all over North America, is considered a roaring success, bringing in social media admiration from pole dancers around the world, known as "Pole Prestige."

However, one hour before this call, I had said my final goodbye to my father as he passed away, his body decimated by an eight-year battle with liver cancer. Holding his hand, I spent the night in the hospital, telling him his daughter was strong and it was okay for him to go to heaven now. As I slept beside him, he exhaled his last breath. The nurse woke me up saying, "Honey… your father is gone."

Listening to the invite to compete, I stared at my father's empty hospital bed. Hearing the news of the upcoming competition, all I could feel was numbness. Heaviness. Shock.

Disconnected, I responded, "Okay. Yeah. You can count on me for a great performance."

To perform well in a pole competition, all your time and energy must be dedicated to training. As a rule, I train a year in advance, with my routine completed three months before competition day. Every day is dedicated to showing up for training sessions—smoothing out the routine, physically memorizing the fine details to the point of madness, where I can feel the movement in every muscle. It's pretty much the dedication you'd expect of any professional dancer or figure skater. While I'm resting from training, I mentally practise by listening to my competition song. When you commit to competing, you are saying yes to dropping all excuses and to training even though your arms are toast, and you are saying goodbye to any personal time for relaxation, in order to float like a feather on competition day. You fight your personal bullshit—thoughts of *I suck* and *So-and-so is better than me*—with a single-minded focus on those three and a half minutes of performance. The physical brutality of competition training—every day you are covered in scratches and bruises, slathering your body with arnica to make the aches bearable—makes absolutely no sense. Yet, to the pole competitor, it's a beloved way of life.

The days after the funeral saw me staring at the pole, knowing I needed to train. And yet my wounded heart made me hide. Instead of reaching for the pole and throwing myself back into training, I stretched for the vodka bottle and escaped into the deceptively loving embrace of alcohol.

The clock ticked on. I lost weeks of training to bingeing. On the days I forced myself to train, my body responded like a slug, lifting itself upside down as though it was weighted down with rocks. I prayed for my training groove to appear, but deep down I knew I had made a mistake.

Still, I pressed on, ignoring that inner voice saying, *Now is not the time to compete. You really should be grieving.* My body became swollen from a combination of alcohol, sugar, and carbs. All the gains from training were cancelled by over-consumption.

Let's Make a Deal

Two weeks before the competition, I made a deal with myself: I'd put the damn bottle away until the competition and then, after, I'd be free to celebrate with a huge glass of champagne. It worked. The choreography flowed and my competition piece was ready for the stage 48 hours before competition day. (Normally, I would have had this down three months earlier.) I ran through the routine—once. Good enough.

Minutes away from stepping onto the competition stage, ready to compete in a costume that barely fit thanks to the aforementioned alcohol, carbs, and sugar, I sent out a text to one of my friends in the audience: "Hey there, when I step off the stage, do me a big favour? Have a glass of champagne and Chambord ready for me? The moment I walk away from the stage, I want that glass in my hand—it's celebration time!"

Standing under the stage lights, ready for "Could Have Been Me" by the Struts to play, I felt alone and disconnected from the audience. The music was fast, but I felt slow. Midway through the piece, a wave of panic flashed through my mind. *I can't remember what I'm doing* was followed by *Just finish this song and get off the stage.*

And as I stepped offstage, the glass of champagne and Chambord was waiting for me like a faithful friend. As I lost myself in the familiar sugar-and-alcohol cloud, standing in line at the bar, I overheard two pole competitors dissecting the performances from my division. I picked up the dreaded reference to "Jane" and the fact that "she sucked." I paid for my fourth glass and retreated to my hotel room.

With every sugar high and alcohol buzz comes the inevitable crash.

It was hard.

Brutal.

Unforgiving.

And it didn't arrive until the next morning, on my flight back to Toronto from Chicago. I had been wide awake for over 24 hours, and the post-competition exhaustion and disappointment mixed with the sugar/alcohol crash finally hit me in the skies between Michigan and Ontario. The result was me throwing up in the airplane's bathroom. I looked like hell and the people on the plane heard every retching sound I made in the tiny lavatory.

I was in full emotional breakdown. To this day, I don't know how I placed at that competition; when the scores came out, I couldn't bring myself to look. The landing created by this fall from grace was a massive splat, and when I got back up, I realized it was time to look at the way I deal with things, and to recognize that I had placed unrealistic expectations on myself. My father had died, and I chose to throw myself into a competition and expected to succeed.

Two years later, after I had allowed myself room to grieve, I felt the need to personally amend my bruised pole ego. The love of pole training returned and I was ready to dive back in. Allowing myself space to play and explore movement, and subsequently becoming re-inspired, I was ready for the challenge of the Toronto Pro Supershow Pole Competition, Masters Division. Embracing the competition journey and thriving with the challenge, I performed my competition piece to "Dig Down" by Muse, feeling fully connected to the audience. I enjoyed a flawless performance and won my division.

When we hit rock bottom, the rise to the top is sweeter.

After Falling Short

As we move through our lives, hiding from disappointment and loss is virtually impossible. Yet we are surprised when we fall short or experience a personal loss and don't know how to deal with it. We brace ourselves against the pain, praying it will go away without us having to dive into its origins and identify the ways we can process it. Knowing and accepting ourselves—our strengths and weaknesses, our hurts and experiences, what makes us tick and why we act the way we do—provides us with the ability to make better choices and decisions in our lives. That way, when we encounter a bump along our life's road, we are better prepared to handle the situation; we don't fall apart or sink into self-destructive modes. We are more graceful and at ease because we have strategies that serve us well. We accept the essence of what makes us different; there is an ease about us, and people around us are drawn in. We become comfortable to be around, because self-awareness brings peace.

We bring energy to every situation, environment, and opportunity. Like the cellphone stashed in our back pocket, we carry our past hurts, experiences, and expectations around with us. Ultimately, we are responsible for understanding ourselves and our behaviours. It's time for some self-discovery.

LET'S DIVE IN. Grab your favourite notebook and start answering these questions.

What do you binge on?

Is it helping you or holding you back? Is it food, alcohol, gossip, FB scrolling, or Netflix?

I get it—I love bingeing on Netflix, and also cat videos! That joyous feeling of completely zoning out on brain candy as a way to relieve stress. However, if you are losing hours to the Kardashians and are unhappy with the direction your life is heading, it's time to rethink the "Netflix and zone out" strategy.

How about your phone? Productive or time-sucking? Are you truly being productive on it, or is it a method to soothe? The day I discovered "Screen Time" on my phone, oh, my heart sank! To see how many hours I spend on my phone was cringe-worthy. Go check out your screen time feature, and whatever you do, don't turn it off! I dare you to keep track of your screen time and celebrate when the reports state you are decreasing your time. Look, I do believe our phones are useful devices as we work our business. But they are also a time-sucking vortex of Instagram (*Dear IG, I love you*). I've mastered the art of looking productive on my phone without truly being fruitful. When our fingers are tapping and scrolling away, we have a feeling of being productive when in reality we are not.

Mindlessly, we turn to coping strategies that may not serve us well—simply as a way to quickly soothe away the stresses. Many times, we're unhappy with the current state of our life but are too exhausted to make changes. So we binge, scroll, and hide because it feels good in the moment. In the long run, though, it doesn't serve us well.

Being a human is messy; we all have "stuff," and we are always figuring it out! We are all dealing with baggage, whether it is childhood trauma, issues, situations, and/or stories that we tell ourselves. Walking wounded, we are figuring out how to heal and move forward in life. Those of us who know we're hurting and understand our past experiences present ourselves differently to the world: we are more graceful and kind to ourselves, because we are doing the work to resolve our pain. We are more self-aware and have come to understand what makes us tick. Armed with self-knowledge, we make better choices and decisions in our lives. It's about living consciously and being mindful.

NOTEBOOK TIME: YOUR TO-DO'S

Write a "Dear Me, I forgive myself for..." letter.

My friend, writing a forgiveness letter to yourself doesn't have to be heavy. Let's make this light and freeing. You can use your notebook or perhaps grab some pretty stationery. When was the last time you grabbed a sheet of quality cardstock with beautiful designs on it? If you're going to write a letter to yourself, make it count with a gold-embossed page.

On the page, with your special pen in hand, begin with "Dear Me, I forgive myself for..." and then, in a steady stream of consciousness, write down whatever comes to your mind. It could be big or small. Forgive yourself for the rules you imposed on yourself. Release yourself from self-judgment that has been holding you back. Have you made mistakes in your life? Welcome to the club! Forgive yourself for those missteps.

Have you fallen into habits of self-soothing bingeing, gossiping, or drama in your life? Recognize your inclination to shift to these habits under stress and say to yourself, "It's okay, I'm becoming more mindful."

What about those moments when you talked yourself out of opportunities and later regretted it? Let it go. Don't beat yourself up for allowing self-doubt to creep in. Forgive yourself. Realize that we allow lack of time and effort, past experiences, and past failures to rent space in our head. Evict those thoughts of self-doubt and cut yourself some slack.

Although time machines haven't been invented (yet), moving forward, we can forgive ourselves for previous missteps. Saying "sorry" to yourself for your past mistakes unshackles you from regret and starts the healing process. By becoming conscious of how you deal with life, you arm yourself to make better decisions when life goes sideways.

At the end of your steady stream of forgiveness consciousness, to give yourself closure, I want you to write: "I forgive myself because I recognize that humans make mistakes. I am human. It's okay to make mistakes. Love, Me."

Don't be surprised if you end up a snotty mess of tears. Leaking tears from your eyes can be healing. Just remember to wear waterproof mascara.

— 8 —

THE
COMPARISON
THIEF

"OUR CLASSES ARE slammed. We are jam-packed!" my competitor proclaimed to the world through their Facebook page status update. While I was sitting in an empty studio, scrolling through Facebook, the feeling of dread settled in my gut. Damn it, her business was doing better than mine.

No matter how hard I tried, I couldn't get people to show up for their classes. There were the usual excuses: "My neck hurts. I'll try another time." "My cat died last month; I am sad." And then my favourite of all time, "Can I just come in and watch the classes?" I was hitting a world of "not right now, maybe later" while it seemed everyone and their best friend was dancing on my competitor's poles.

My entrepreneurial ass was being handed to me.

I felt like my business was failing.

I felt like I was failing.

Months later, I learned my competitor was experiencing the same hell as I was—the nos, the "maybe next month"s and "oh, it looks too hard"s—and that she was stretching the truth as a way to market her business. She was making it appear that every pole had bodies on it—yet she was facing similar rejection.

I allowed comparison to slice through my identity as a business owner, and I began to sink into the abyss of "I suck and everyone is better than me." Visiting "Comparison-ville" landed me in a funk that lasted for weeks. Decisions I made were coming from the perspective of "everyone else is doing better than me"—when in reality we were all trying to do our best.

I wasn't the only one living in Comparison-ville.

Nicole, 38 years old, had it all—loving husband, two kids, a beautiful house. She and her husband were both employed and didn't worry about finances. But she always felt that her friend Carol was living a better life. A more exciting life—her "best ever" life!

Carol was going on wine tours. She had beach vacations. She was going to the newest restaurants.

How did Nicole know about Carol's adventures? She was following her Instagram feed—a curated, idyllic version of Carol's life.

After Nicole put her little girls to bed, put on her favourite comfortable onesie pyjamas, and curled up on the couch with her phone, she would peer into Carol's #amazinglife and sink into a feeling of lack. She wasn't living an interesting existence! Instead of cheering her on, Nicole secretly wanted Carol to fail so that she could feel better about herself.

Carol did have a different life than Nicole. She was single, had no kids, and was attached to her career. She was experiencing life differently, and wasn't posting about the days she felt overwhelmed. She was only posting the highlights of her life and passing over the lowlights.

And Nicole was interpreting it as "her life is so much better than mine."

Over a glass of wine, Nicole confessed to her friend about her jealousy. In her mind, her life was routine and repetitive while Carol's seemed adventurous. To her surprise, Carol confessed to her that she was drowning in debt and struggling to find calm.

Our curated social media unrealness gives the impression that our lives are perfect, when in fact that is rarely true. When we only post our successes and not our struggles, it hits the "I'm not good enough" button. We spend too much time in Comparison-ville, and we end up measuring our lives against others'—thinking that someone's bank account is larger than ours or that their business is more profitable or their house is nicer. It steals from our heart and hurts our soul, creating a me-versus-you mentality. It pushes us into a place of insecurity, pulling away our power and zapping our confidence.

I see this often in pole classes, where a student compares their pole moves to another student's ability. Instead of recognizing that everybody (and every body) is different, they feel resentful when someone achieves a pole move before them. It's guaranteed that student will end up quitting the sport, because they fall into the pit of self-judgment.

Never compare the exterior of someone else's life with the interior of your own.

We truly have no idea what is happening in other people's lives. When we compare our current state with the outward appearance of another's life... we are doomed. Our self-esteem takes a beating. We create stories in our head about how much better someone else has it in their life. Right now, that person could be looking at your life and thinking that it is better than theirs!

Everyone has circumstances, struggles, and obstacles to navigate. Wounds to heal and disappointments to face. It's easy to get trapped into thinking a different person has a sweeter path. This can be a default mode that helps us defend why we are struggling: "I'm frustrated because so-and-so has it all." This victim thinking does not serve us well and holds us back from truly facing why we are unhappy in our life.

In the article "Social Comparison, Social Media, and Self-Esteem," Erin A. Vogel, Jason P. Rose, Lindsay R. Roberts, and Katheryn Eckles from the University of Toledo researched Midwestern college students, their Facebook use, and how they compare themselves through viewing others' Facebook profiles. The researchers suggest there is a detrimental effect on well-being from frequent Facebook comparisons. They encourage Facebook users to be mindful of their mental health because of the implications of Facebook comparisons. In the beginning of the COVID-19 pandemic, during lockdown, the phenomenon of social media comparison was on steroids. How many banana/wheat/sourdough bread pics did you see on Instagram? Then, over on TikTok, it seemed everyone was doing the "Blinding Lights" challenge (myself included). If you weren't posting about learning a new skill or language, creating art, AND taking an online university course, you weren't "enough" while the world dived into a major crisis.

Then there's the meme "Bored in the house? In 1665, the University of Cambridge temporarily closed due to the bubonic plague. As a result, Isaac Newton had to work from home. He used the time to develop calculus and the theory of gravity." Good grief. This Canva-created, simplified version of Isaac Newton's genius sets people up for failure. During a global pandemic, if all you focused on was drinking water, wearing fresh clothes, eating a carrot stick, having a good night's sleep, social distancing, and wearing a mask—you did great!

It's time to steal back from the Comparison Thief and focus on our own lives, without the lens of social media. In *Psychology Today*'s article "The Comparison Trap," Rebecca Webber suggests we examine how our social media behaviours contribute to our relationships. Instead of measuring ourselves against others, we can choose to rebuild our self-confidence. We grow through connection and celebrate our friends' successes. We know that success is abundant—there are no limits.

After falling into the comparison trap of checking out my competitors' social media, I learned to "never compare the interior of your business to the exterior of others'." This reframing of my mindset led me to understand that my competitors' success doesn't mean my business will fail. We can all be successful and shine together.

NOTEBOOK TIME: YOUR TO-DO'S (PART 1)

How do we get to the place where we are no longer comparing ourselves with others and sucking the joy from our day?

Mute or snooze the triggering profile.

With our morning cup of coffee in hand, we scroll through Facebook out of habit or simply to see what is going on in the world. Then it happens... Jessica uploaded images of her recent amazing adventure. Or Sarah's posted a humble brag of the "I am so blessed" variety. A feeling of anger and resentment swells and we bitterly swallow that morning cup of joe—and for the next 15 minutes we envision destruction and demise for our friends.

Hello! You have been triggered!

Let's face it, there are humans in our lives who provoke a strong reaction within us. I am sure they are wonderful, sweet, and loving people! They love puppy dogs, eat healthy, and always seem to be doing the right things. Unknowingly, they trigger a reaction within us. It's not their fault! It's OUR responsibility to identify our triggers. Figure out WHY you freaked out. What was it about the status update/pic/video that prompted you to plot that person's downfall? Did their post hit your "I'm not good enough" button?

Fact is, you too have been unfollowed. You have been placed on mute. You have been snoozed.

I've been unfollowed because of #SundayBumday.

What's Sunday Bumday, you ask? It is a global pole dancer "thing." Every Sunday, pole dancers will post a Facebook or Instagram pic of their bottom and tag it #SundayBumday. It's a form of rebellion. At the time of writing this book, there are 492,330 posts under this hashtag on Instagram alone. I adore Sunday Bumday for the sheer naughtiness of it.

Did you know that, at one point, Facebook showed your friends which posts you liked? Well, I learned the hard way. Every Sunday, drinking my morning coffee, I'd check out the hashtag and click the heart as a way to say, "Tee-hee, I'm celebrating Sunday Bumday with you!" Little did I know, as I showed my support, that the posts would show up on my other friends' feeds, including Joanne's FB News Feed. Joanne was NOT a fan of Sunday Bumday. Apparently, she didn't want to see people's bums as she sipped her morning tea. Hence, I was unfollowed over my love of Sunday Bumday. At first I felt judged, but my love of Sunday Bumday helped me overcome the feeling of rejection!

Deep inside you, get in touch with your heart and examine the reasons for your feelings of inferiority. Heal those feelings of inadequacy so that you can genuinely cheer your friends on.

Don't Compare Your Beginning to the Middle of Someone's Journey

The stage lights were shining bright as I took my final pose in front of the electrifying crowd at Mod Club in Toronto. I finished performing to "Madness" by Muse, for the sold-out "Girlesque 2013" event hosted by Great Canadian Burlesque. The club was standing room only, with no space to move, even to get to the bar. As I held my end pose—the Superman (just like Superman flying through the air, but on a pole, legs straight back, pole between them, one arm extended out in front, the other holding the pole)—I looked out to the audience and all eyes were on me. Months of rehearsals had been dedicated to creating a flawless pole performance, and I'd nailed it! Every move, look, and extension was on point, and I was feeling the exhilaration of hard work and preparation that had paid off. My hands were grippy (when you perform pole, grippy hands are preferable to sweaty ones) and every pole move hit the electronic rock beat.

Wearing my black Swarovski-covered pole top and bottom (I named my costume Black Sparkle Magic!), I stepped off my pole stage (a portable stage with a base and a free-standing pole) and took my bow to thank the audience and accept their applause. As the curtain closed, I stepped over to the wings to steady my heart and soak in the experience.

One of the other burlesque performers, a young girl dressed in a gorgeous lilac corset and fishnets, strutted up. "Oh my god, that was amazing! That move you did, upside down, with your leg out! What's it called?"

I glowed. "That's my favourite move! It's an Extended Butterfly!"

"What a beautiful name! I want to learn that! Can I?" she squealed.

I felt butterflies of excitement, because I love teaching pole, especially when it's my favourite moves.

"Of course. Start with beginner classes and work your way up. It'll be fun!"

Lowering her eyes, she sighed. "How long would it take me to learn? I need to be amazing so I can add pole to my performances too."

Comparison Thief alert. To master the Extended Butterfly, you need to hold your body weight and be able to go upside down comfortably and push your body away from the pole. It takes months.

"Sign up and let's work towards achieving this move." I handed her my business card.

Two weeks later, she showed up for her first beginner class. It ended up being her last.

Since she hadn't worked out for years and her upper body strength was in need of conditioning, her expectations of perfection didn't match the reality. She could hold herself up on the pole for two seconds and wasn't ready to go upside down. (It's rare for anyone to go upside down in their first pole class. In fact, as an instructor, I rarely advise it.) Frustrated, she demanded her money back. Disappointed that she lacked patience, I gave her a refund.

When we begin a new journey—a business, weight loss, a life change—it's messy. We struggle and learn along the way. Most beginnings are bumpy. We feel uncomfortable, uncertain, and overwhelmed. Learning something new feels difficult and forces us to stretch. And when we see someone who is more seasoned with their skills—perhaps in the middle or latter part of their journey—we automatically feel inferior and may opt to give up. Had this aspiring pole dancing burlesque performer been able to see the beginnings of my pole career, when I had no upper body strength, couldn't touch my toes or climb the pole, perhaps she would have continued. If you feel a real need to compare—to scratch that itch—look at the person's beginnings. Their evolution will put everything into perspective—and show you a road map towards success.

"Eyes On Your Own Page" Cue

When you peer over the desk of someone else's life, remind yourself, "Eyes on your own page!" Remember back in our school days, during a test or exam, if you were sitting close to another student and were unsure of the answer, your eyes would kinda scan across the desk and then you would hear your teacher announce to the room, "Just a reminder to keep your eyes on your own page!" Use this as a cue for yourself. When we feel the need to check out someone's Facebook or Instagram as a way to see how we measure up... "Eyes on your own page!" Close the tabs and put your eyes back on your own page.

"Celebrate a Friend's Success"

Let's open our hearts to be happy for other people's accomplishments and successes, to genuinely feel excitement and joy as our friends reach their goals. By doing so, we feel the happiness they are currently feeling—realizing that success and joy are abundant. When we are surrounded by joy, fulfillment, and happiness—we begin to join in. When a friend's "look at what I achieved" IG or Facebook post pops up, click the heart and leave a comment cheering them on. Success is limitless and contagious!

NOTEBOOK TIME: YOUR TO-DO'S (PART 2)

Update your evidence file. Remember the "I'm a Rock Star" file I talked about in chapter three? Are you keeping it up? When was the last time you added to your file? Take a moment to go through your emails, messages, images, and videos, and update your file.

In those moments when you feel the Comparison Thief sliding in to steal your joy and make you feel like shit—turn to your "I'm a Rock Star" evidence file. The concrete proof will remind you of your awesomeness in those evil moments of self-doubt and self-sabotage.

— 9 —

HANDLE
WITH
SELF-CARE

LLOW ME TO introduce "Lead Foot Louise" and the moment she saw the flashing lights in her rear-view mirror. As soon as she saw those red, blue, and white lights, she knew that her time was up and she had been caught. There was no way out of this one.

This queen of overcommitment loved to cram as much into her day as possible, racing in and out of events, trying to be everywhere—being seen and making connections to ensure she never missed out on any opportunity that crossed her path. Zipping from place to place—home to work to events to after-school activities, always in a state of anxiety—she believed speed was her friend. With her foot pressing hard on the gas pedal, she stared forward at the road—her thoughts racing, heart pounding in her chest as she beat the clock so she wasn't "that mom" who was always late at pickup.

Recently, she had launched a new business and desperately wanted to be a success—no matter the cost. This haunted her thoughts.

The hustle.

The grind.

No rest for the wicked.

She fed off the adrenalin, while her fear of failure and willingness to risk it all fuelled the engine. This was her drug.

Deep down, the heavy feeling—an unhappy and disappointed state—created chaos in her life, and speeding was a symptom. In that moment, her lack of self-control attracted the attention of a livid police officer, who was now leading her to the back of a police cruiser. She had been caught barrelling down the highway at 160 kilometres (100 miles) per hour, more than 50 kph (30 mph) over the speed limit. In Canada, this is known as stunt driving, and it is rewarded with the highest level of speeding ticket issued. Fines can range up to $10,000, with seven days' impoundment of vehicle, potential jail time, licence suspension, and six demerit points.

She was screwed. The car she was driving? It belonged to her husband.

Holy. Shit.

Sitting in the back of the police cruiser, her eyes burned with tears as she watched the tow truck leave with her husband's car, headed for the impound lot. Louise wondered if this was her rock bottom moment. Facing potential jail time, suspension of her licence, and an overwhelming fine, she asked herself, *Can it get any worse from here?* Oh yes, it could! She had to face her husband and tell him about his car. THAT is worse than jail time.

Since it was her first incident of (getting caught) speeding, the officer chose to send her home in a taxi, and she didn't have to spend a night in jail. With no driver's licence for seven days, a stunt driving charge, and a court date in hand, Louise walked into her house ready to come clean with her husband.

"Babe, I'm in trouble... and it involved your car." She sank to the ground in a wave of exhaustion, tears, and uncertainty. The weight of her inability to take care of herself had led to a disastrous result, and now she had to face the music. This wasn't solely about being caught, it was the fact that she was driving dangerously, with little regard for the health and safety of other drivers.

After the dust settled, Louise and her husband worked out a plan to help her slow down and revise how she cared for her well-being. It began with rethinking her relationship with self-care.

Resting had always been an afterthought, something she would eventually get to—maybe one day—perhaps at the end of the week. Being a focused and determined person, she planned every aspect of her day with zero wiggle room. Taking time out for herself was viewed as a distraction from getting results in her business; that time could be dedicated to emails, networking, planning, making videos, creating sales offers, and working with clients. She bargained with herself: "When I reach a 15 percent increase in my sales, then I will treat myself to a massage." But when she reached that 15 percent increase, she would bump it up to 20 percent, never settling long enough to hit pause and refresh herself. And now her inability to take care of herself had led to a disastrous result.

In the book *The Resilient Practitioner: Burnout Prevention and Self-Care Strategies for Counselors, Therapists, Teachers, and Health Professionals*, Thomas M. Skovholt and Michelle Trotter-Mathison discuss how the giving of oneself is a constant requirement for success. When we are constantly giving our energy and depleting our reserves, we lead ourselves to burnout from the inside out. But you can understand and use self-care as a form of self-preservation that will lead you towards success.

We initiate self-care methods to keep ourselves healthy and tackle our days. However, instead of viewing self-care as a tool for health and success, as a way to take care of ourselves while we work towards achieving our goals, many of us use it as a reward system and burn ourselves to a crisp in the meantime. We force ourselves to wait to feel good, until disaster strikes and we end up face down in the gutter, spent and in crisis. We tend to use self-care as a luxury, a present to ourselves—so that we have to prove our worthiness before we take care of ourselves. But then we end up burning out, barely dragging ourselves across the finish line. This approach is reflected in our work and overall attitude. Instead of celebrating our victories at work, we feel disappointed, exhausted, and empty.

Self-Care Isn't Selfish

In the craziness of our day-to-day lives, we carve out moments as opportunities to reconnect with our well-being. To stay tuned up and strong.

Self-care is a necessity, not a reward. It is a way to keep ourselves at our best, so that we are proud of our work and maintain a high self-worth all along. To do this, we should weave self-care throughout our day, using strategies to stay fuelled all the way along our journey.

We can be fierce, strong, and beautiful and remember to take moments to be kind to ourselves—moments of self-love. The version of our best happens when we are taking care of ourselves.

In my podcast *Reclaim Your Spark*—episode "A Simple Way to Add Self Care Everyday"—I interviewed Melissa Joy Olson, owner of Euphoria Studio, a spa and beauty boutique in Frenchtown, New Jersey. Melissa has spent her entire career helping women see themselves as beautiful, strong, loving, and capable. Always reminding others that "you can't pour from an empty cup," she has planted her flag on loving ourselves and creating moments of care. Embedded in her memory is witnessing her grandmother creating self-care rituals throughout the day. As a child raised by her grandparents, she noticed—even among the bustle of the day, which included caring for Melissa, making meals, and maintaining the home—that her grandmother would take a special moment for herself. Towards the end of the afternoon, up in her bedroom, her grandmother would change her clothes, fix her hair and makeup, and take a moment to gaze at her reflection. Little Melissa, peeking around the door frame, caught the eye of her grandmother.

"Why are you staring at yourself?" Melissa inquired.

"Because it makes me feel good." Her grandmother smiled.

This moment left a lasting impression on Melissa, who now, as a busy entrepreneur raising four children, has her own self-care rituals. Sometimes it's lighting a candle in the evening and feeling gratitude for the day, or it might be taking a 15-minute walk midday as a way to reset.

On Instagram, I posted "Self-care is not luxury" and asked, "What are you doing to care for yourself so that you don't burn out?"

Some of the answers I received:

- "Sitting by an open window and breathing in the fresh air."

- "I took the day off on Monday and lay down for the whole day."

- "I've been taking a quiet time out in the evenings to just be still and enjoy nature."

- "Self-care is vital! For me it's spending time in my yard."

- "I get up early to pray and have quiet time every day. I find practising gratitude helps blow away the blahs."

- "Meditation and bubble baths."

Leaving Lead Foot Behind

Let's return to Lead Foot Louise.

Standing in her hallway, unable to look at her husband, Louise confessed to the stunt driving charge, and the potential jail time, and the $10,000 fine, and "Oh, yes... I got your car impounded," she whispered.

"What? What the hell?" he questioned, realizing that his wife was struggling and in epic crisis mode. He knew he could either condemn or problem-solve in this situation. Thankfully, he chose the latter. He reached out his arms to hold his wife as she fell apart.

With his car impounded and her licence suspended for a week, he used her vehicle while she stayed home to care for her well-being. Together, they worked out a plan to help her find peace, feel in control, and replace her frantic energy with calmness. Doing so meant strategically doing less, no longer saying yes to everything; hiring more staff for her business; and dedicating one full day each week to no work. She discovered a new-found love for Sundays as her non-biz day.

When her licence suspension was completed, she began planning her appointments with extra time between them— giving herself some "wiggle room" for travel.

With the help of a therapist and the support of her family, Louise learned how to properly schedule her time, came to understand how fear and anxiety drove her to chaos, and reframed self-care as a battery recharge rather than a reward.

At her court date, her lawyer demonstrated the changes she had made in her life, and her ticket was reduced to a regular speeding ticket with a manageable fine.

She used self-care as a way to take a rest spot along the entrepreneurial journey.

By saying no to chaos and becoming mindful, she felt more successful and fulfilled, because she was now in control. She designed her life like a well-planned GPS route. Her business revenue increased because she was present and aware.

She settled down in her life, her family started to thrive—and to this day she has not received another speeding ticket.

BY NOW, you may be wondering if this is a fictionalized or composite character designed to illustrate a point. I promise you, it is not.

Plot twist: I am Lead Foot Louise.

My middle names are Natalie Louise, and the nickname was created by my husband to illustrate how scattered and "on the go" I was. (He also had another nickname, NASCAR Natalie, but Lead Food Louise was the more popular one.) The chaotic period was between 2008 and 2010, coinciding with the opening of my pole dancing studio. Anxiety and the drive for success fuelled my behaviour of epic rushing and scatteredness, forcing me to the brink of exhaustion.

On that fateful day when it all came to a grinding halt, I found myself in the back of a police cruiser. I was wearing killer black Mary Jane stilettos, my favourite black leather miniskirt, and the coolest patterned tights. Part of me wondered if my outfit would help get me out of the ticket. No dice. And by the way, there's little space in the back of a cruiser! Not only did I feel like the worst mom ever for being late for pickup, but I also had to pull my knees up to my chest, folding myself in half—and cementing the feeling of being a complete fuck-up.

Thanks to a good lawyer and an excellent driving record (because I hadn't been caught before) I was lucky to receive no jail time, only a reduced fine. Oh, and I paid out thousands of dollars in legal fees and therapy bills. Now I'm the Queen of Cruise Control and driving under the speed limit. (My apologies to the cars behind me!)

═══ **NOTEBOOK TIME:** YOUR TO-DO'S ═══

Time to determine if you are weaving self-care into your day. Take a look at these questions and use them to formulate your Self-Care Action Plan.

- Throughout the day, are you hydrating and nourishing your body with healthy food and drink?

- Do you avoid racing around?

- Do you end your day with a self-care ritual?

- Are you exercising throughout the week?

- Do you allow time to rest?

- Are you mindful of your eating habits?

- Do you place boundaries on who receives your energy?

Now, if you answered no to any of these questions, that's a perfect place to start making changes. Start turning those nos into yesses.

Feeling bored with your current self-care rituals? Feel free to use some of mine:

- Read a book, on a blanket under a big tree.

- Go for a manicure and a pedicure.

- Sit still and chill—not playing on your phone, just chilling out and sitting still.

- Take a leisurely walk—not a walk with purpose, but a walk filled with calm and dreamy energy.

- Sunday Home Spa Night is so much fun. Put on a facial mask, throw some Epsom salts into your bathtub for a soak, and chill.

- Netflix and veg out.

- Take a nap. (I am a champion napper!)

- Order in dinner from your favourite restaurant.

- Check out an online art gallery to fill your creative spirit.

- Colouring—yes! Drawing and colouring. Takes us back to our childhood, and it is so meditative.

- Take a mental health day—a full day to do whatever you want!

- Move your body. Find an activity that moves your body in many ways. Play and have fun.

- Go to bed early. This is a trick in itself for me, because I tend to delay my bedtime.

- Say no! Just say no! (Or use "let me think about that" as a buffer.)

Remember, taking a moment for yourself is not an act of selfishness. By honouring your energy, using your Self-Care Action Plan to recharge, you are better able to handle difficulties and pressure. The magic begins when you devote time to yourself. Give yourself a plethora of self-care habits to add variety to your week—you'll be fresh, engaged, and rested.

— 10 —

MOVE
TO FEEL
GOOD

URPEES DON'T LIKE You Anyway!

This is a saying on a tank top, and it's not wrong!

Have you heard of the Burpee Challenge? It's taking the burpee, a full-body exercise popularized by the United States Armed Forces, and performing the exercises 50 times a day for 30 days.

Seriously, for 30 days, it's 50 burpees every single day. Every single freakin' day. Starting in a squat, placing hands on the ground so you can jump back into a plank. Then drop into a push-up and spring your feet back into a squat to standing position. For a whole month. Essentially, doing a dreaded activity 1,500 times. (Lord help you if it's a 31-day month. If you take the challenge, choose February—it's only 28 days.)

However, the idea of a well-toned, muscular body by Day 30 is too much to resist. So, on the first day of the challenge, a person knocks off 50 burpees ... sweats, breathes hard, feels like vomiting. Checkmark, Day 1 challenge is done.

Day 2 and back at it, another 50. The metallic taste floods your mouth due to pushing too hard.

By Day 3, "Fitness Challenge Dropout" is looking like an inevitability.

(An aside: Did you know that burpees were developed by an American physiologist named Royal Burpee? What a brilliant name! Royal. Burpee. With a name like that, his contribution to the fitness industry was meant to be! But I digress ...)

For over 10 years, I have taught in the fitness industry and witnessed the "I'm starting a new fitness routine" excitement.

"Yes! I'm going to get into the best shape of my life!" a new client exclaims as they sign up for their membership, that euphoric high that comes with making the decision to change your physical body.

Within a few weeks, as the realization of continued effort settles in, the life-changing excitement screeches to a halt. In order to get into the best shape of our lives, we have to *show up* to our workouts.

We set ourselves up for these impossible challenges, feeling the initial gung-ho, then day by day we start to abandon our plan. Life derails us. One of the kids gets sick, there's a leak in the basement, we have a headache, our friend wants to go out, our work demands more of our time, we go on a trip, or the glow of our laptop sucks us into a funk. It is virtually impossible to finish, and we end up feeling disappointed in ourselves. We failed. Again.

Time to simplify our workouts to bring success into our lives and break free from the over-the-top fitness challenges. Let's clean this up.

To feel vibrant and excited about life, we need to move our bodies. That's it.

It doesn't need to be a major event, an epic challenge, or a groundbreaking initiative.

Movement is the catalyst. Bringing physical action into our lives creates momentum and gets our creative juices flowing. It generates energy that not only shifts our bodily appearance but has a trickle-down effect by giving us drive and momentum.

According to the *American Journal of Preventive Medicine*, any level of physical activity, including low levels such as walking, can prevent depression. Physical activity will serve as a valuable mental health strategy—a powerful tool to help you feel more vibrant, happy, and confident. Because the more we sit around, the more tired we become. The less we engage our muscles, the further we sink into darkness. When we start moving, we are revving up the power generator that courses through our veins and makes us feel unstoppable! Break out of that rut, move, and become unstuck!

Build Up by Starting Simple

That's how one of my clients, Anna, revived her energy. The devastation of losing her job sent her to the couch, where she stayed for months. Her body created an indentation in the cushion, contributing to a cozy, soothing, hide-from-the-world existence that opened the door for depression to settle in. On top of that, she became immersed in the world of Facebook, scrolling through post after post. Some nights, instead of going to bed, she would drift off into her body-enveloping couch with her phone in her hand. The tiredness had taken over and it was difficult to shake.

She was Facebook friends with a lot of active people who would post their marathon pics, their workout videos, the status update "Just ran 10 miles before work," and although publicly she liked their posts, gave them the thumbs-up, secretly she loathed their posts because she couldn't fathom how to go from a couch to a marathon. One by one, she started to unfollow her active friends because their posts made her feel lazy. Screw them!

The pivotal moment occurred when she visited her friend's FB page and saw the image of her friends out on a day's excursion up a mountain, looking fresh-faced and laughing. How dare they cast her aside and not invite her! She probably would have turned down the invitation anyway. But now she knew she was missing out, and the realization made her wonder: *How do I go from living in couch-land to a day-long hiking adventure up a mountain?*

You break it down, one step at a time. Or, in Anna's case, it became one song at a time.

Out of desperation, she found the middle ground, the bridge from the couch to the uphill climb. One afternoon, she decided, "I'm going to just dance around for three songs."

She grabbed her phone, threw on some music, and danced around her house. She felt silly. Her joints ached. Her body felt hot and she smelled sweaty. Her face turned red as she moved to the music. And... she felt better.

For two weeks, she followed a "Dance It Out" morning routine. She created a special playlist on Spotify and danced around her house to feel energized. Her playlist was filled with explicit-lyric songs ("Get Up, Get Out" by Born Dirty featuring Jstlbby). This morning dance-off evaporated her depression and she started to feel joy again.

One morning, after an epic "Dance It Out," she sent a message to her friend: "For your next outdoor excursion, please think of me as an invite. I miss everyone so much." And with that, she decimated her isolation cocoon and re-entered her community.

Sometimes we get knocked down and retreat. To rise back up, we need to consistently show up for simple steps. We don't need exaggerated challenges to make the shift; a daily "Dance It Out" to swear-laden beats could be all it takes.

Following Through

Sometimes, putting on workout clothes is an act of bravery in itself. Which is why my focus on fitness has nothing to do with losing weight and is more about following through on our intentions to feel strong and capable, showing up, and using movement as a way to feel good and embrace our bodies regardless of the numbers on the scale. The best way to set ourselves up for success is to adopt a playful mentality towards an active lifestyle.

Make it playtime, my friend!

When we flip the switch from blood, sweat, and other fluids to fun, laughter, and play, we are more apt to show up, to grab our workout clothes as we run out the door to our fitness class because we don't want to miss a beat!

This is one of the reasons boutique-like fitness studios sprang up and thrived. They became a place (physical or online) to let loose, toss aside ego, joke around, play, and realize "Whoops! I worked out too!" They offer a playful, rebellious opportunity to make friends, be accepted for who you are (inclusivity is a MUST), and even reinvent yourself. Add some glitter and badass workout gear and you have the ingredients for a successful workout adventure!

Exciting Workouts

People look for novelty in their workouts as a way to stay engaged. At the time pole dancing entered the fitness industry, the focus was on Curves, big-box gyms like Gold's Gym, and Jazzercise. Other sports that took off due to the novelty and intrigue include hot yoga (you are surrounded by sweaty humans, in a stifling, humid room set to 43°C (110°F)... and you LOVE it!); aerial yoga (suspended in the air with fabric, like a butterfly); goat yoga (downward-dogging it as kids start to climb on top of you); and even spin (what started out as a group cycling class became this DJ-fuelled party experience with lights and laughter). Got a chair? With a hair flip and a hip circle, this household object becomes your dance partner, in an activity known as chair dancing.

What's going to be your "intriguing" way of getting in shape? The type of thing that makes you count down the clock until it's time to play? Investing your time and energy in a playful form of fitness brings in those "feel-good vibes" that we love to welcome into our lives.

Let's challenge the "I don't have time to work out" whimper.

It's not that you don't have time; you just haven't found a workout that gives you the adrenalin rush. Prior to grabbing the pole, between the ages of 19 and 33, I was sedentary. As a former dance kid, I left the tap shoes in my childhood closet and dedicated my time to building a career. My barrier to exercise was my undivided attention to being successful in my nine-to-five job, which left me exhausted and gaining weight. Becoming a success in my field was forefront, leaving no room for anything else. Slowly, burnout settles in and life becomes miserable. Finding a fun activity, such as pole, relit my pilot light. I made time for classes, and became intrigued with body conditioning and flexibility exercises (all for the glory of pole, of course!).

In the 2003 *Health Education Research* study "When More Is Better: Number of Motives and Reasons for Quitting as Correlates of Physical Activity in Women," Cheryl B. Anderson finds loss of interest to be one of the top barriers to maintaining dedication, creating physical exercise dropouts. Enjoyable programs help remove those obstacles, leading to continual participation.

Perhaps you're doing workouts that leave you feeling awkward and uncomfortable? When we have a way to train that makes us feel like a superstar, we will make time! The chore will dissolve, and be replaced by a Marvel-like surge that leads us to our superhero stance as we flex our muscles. We will make time to feel this power because we can't live without it. We will whip out our phone, swipe over to our calendar, and schedule our superhero training session. Our workout priority will jump ahead of time-wasting activities as we end up valuing our wellness and celebrating along the way—celebrating that we showed up, played, and are now enjoying our post-workout bliss. Each time, we honour our effort and cheer ourselves on—reminding ourselves that we are worth the effort and fun that comes from building up our mental and physical strength. You rock star!

To further boost your rock star vibe, why not add some cool tunes to your workout? Hearing the dance beat of a song that lifts and energizes you, it's as though a DJ has created a soundtrack to your workout that makes you break into a John Travolta *Saturday Night Fever* strut. Adding this ingredient will propel you off the couch and get you moving! Looking for some cool beats to move to? I've got your back—DJ Jane to the rescue! Add these to your playlist:

- "Stupid Love" by Lady Gaga
- "Give Me Your Love" by Sigala (feat. John Newman and Nile Rodgers)
- "Timber" by Pitbull (feat. Kesha)
- Anything by Kesha (Yes, I have a Kesha obsession...)
- "Bang Bang" by Jessie J, Ariana Grande, and Nicki Minaj
- "Shake It Off" by Taylor Swift

Look for a workout that is thrilling; something that grabs your attention. Look around and see what is out there in your community. If you immediately think to yourself, *I could never do that*—that's the workout to try! An exciting workout program guides you out of your comfort zone and shakes off monotony. Don't just settle for the treadmill; look for something new and adventurous to keep yourself engaged.

1 Sign up for it and show up.

It is better to pay for the class; you are more apt to show up when your dollars have been spent in holding the spot. If it's a free class, your commitment level is low. As a studio owner, trust me—I've seen the commitment level of the "free class student." They are more likely to cancel or not show up than students who have paid. Also, when you pay for a class, you honour the business owner's hard work and commitment in providing quality experiences. It takes dollars to run a quality program, and our community is stronger when local businesses thrive.

2 Support your local fitness studio.

During the COVID-19 pandemic, fitness businesses were one of the hardest-hit industries, with studios and gyms shutting down throughout the country. Making a profit in fitness is challenging enough at the best of times; add a pandemic and lockdowns, and small business owners lose hope and faith. Lend them support by buying a gift certificate, prepaying for classes, joining their online programs, leaving positive Google reviews, and sharing details of their business with your friends. (Actually, these practices are appreciated at all times—global pandemic or not.)

3 Celebrate every time you move your body.
You did it! You fought against the tendency to quit. The deadlines and demands were put on the shelf, while you dedicated time to yourself. Work can wait when you prioritize your health.

Actions, repeated over and over again, will bring results that make us feel stronger and healthier and exude confidence. Choosing joyful activities will help us make the switch from seeing training as a challenge to experiencing it as play. When we do so, we will show up more often in our lives.

— 11 —

THE
POWER OF
THE SUNDAY
PLANNING
SESSION

M Y SWAROVSKI PEN glides across the page as I write about my latest hopes and wishes. This crystal-covered instrument feels magical, as though it has the divine ability to launch my dreams and turn them into reality. As I empty out my thoughts into my notebook, the steam rises from my cup of tea, and the living room in my tiny home expands with abundant energy. For the last four years, this bliss-filled ritual—my secret weapon—has transformed my life from ungrounded romanticism to "I am capable" actualization.

Before I began this practice, I was winging it and fighting an internal boxing match. Although leaving my career as a preschool teacher and opening a pole dancing studio seemed like a fabulous life change, I couldn't escape the feeling of impending doom.

You know that feeling when you lean back in your chair and start to fall backwards? The "backwards chair fall" feeling was never-ending; the rapid heartbeat, the dizziness with tingles down my arm, began as soon as the sun rose. I was reacting to every situation in complete crisis mode and spinning my wheels ("Oh shit! I haven't paid the hydro bill in months! That's why it's shut off!"). The studio, now always busy and active, was overwhelming, and my "go to" was to duck and hide. One unforeseen calamity after another would arise. I felt stuck, a feeling that landed on my shoulders like a heavy bag that I carried wherever I went.

Around my home.

To bed with me.

To the coffee shop.

To other people's houses.

My back and heart would ache due to this weighted bag of worries and disappointment.

As I drove to the studio, the "Bag of Angst" would be flung on the seat beside me. Tears would fall down my face as my mind sank into the rabbit hole of "my life sucks and there is nothing I can do about it." I would carry this bulk while I walked my dog, thinking how absolutely lucky he was because he didn't have this so-called "curse" that I had—the torment of knowing there was more for me in life but struggling against restlessness and gloom.

I had always been an ungrounded dreamer—someone whose head was always in the clouds, conjuring up ideas but not knowing how to implement them—but then the realization hit me over the head: no one is going to save me. How I wanted someone to swoop in, see my greatness, wave their magical wand, and transform my life into an endless stream of Veuve Clicquot moments. Damn it—the rescue mission was taking forever! *Hurry up*, I pleaded. *I am sinking in regret.*

"Please save me," I shouted to the stars above. Silence was always the response. For 10 minutes I would stand in the emptiness of the night.

Slowly, a whispering realization started to grow louder: *If it's to be, it's up to me.* The Hot Mess HAD to become the Hot Champion of Saving Herself—taking charge and assuming responsibility for her life. The tipping point arrived during my annual physical, when my doctor inquired, "How are you?" and I crumbled into a puddle of tears. I admitted the sheer daily dread.

"Have you considered you might have a generalized anxiety disorder? With your maternal manic depression history, your brain chemistry and hormones are more likely to struggle than someone without mental illness lineage," she suggested, reaching for her writing pad. "Here's a referral to a therapist who specializes in anxiety. Give your mind a break. This therapist will help you create strategies to settle down."

Wow. Never had I realized that this constant feeling of doom and failure could be the result of an undiagnosed mental illness. The doctor's words "give your mind a break" became a relieving mantra as I made the decision to investigate the possibility that I had an anxiety disorder.

Taking the Advice of Others

I decided to take my doctor's advice. Seeing the therapist worked out very well, in fact. The therapist suggested that, instead of winging it, I should start planning my weeks. This would help my feeling of being lost or helpless, as I would know what I expected of myself and exactly what I needed to accomplish in the days ahead.

I flung that heavy bag of shitty angst down to the side and, just like Beyoncé in the "Crazy in Love" video (where she swaggers down the street wearing her jean booty shorts, white tank top, and some fine red pumps), I flipped my hair and strutted away. Google it—Beyoncé's "Crazy in Love" official video from 2003. Trust me, you will feel the power in this song.

So began my Sunday Planning Sessions.

Planning grounds you. It's taking your dreams, writing them down on paper, and breaking them down into actionable steps. It's translating the wish of "I want to make more money" into "This is how I am going to make more money." It's writing your thoughts, dreams, and goals down, and then adding the "how" to them, which will push your energy forward.

Action creates momentum.

I love to dream—don't get me wrong! Oh, how I love the feeling of dreaming. In order to make those dreams happen, though, we have to create a road map—"this is how I'm going to do it" actionable steps. By getting out of your head, you bring life into your dreams.

Sunday Planning Sessions have helped me:

- Transform my home from crazy and messy, a place I would never invite someone to because I was embarrassed, into a haven of order, beauty, and love

- Pull my pole dancing business out of terrible financial clutter, with two years' worth of disorganized bookkeeping, into a financial system that was efficient and easy

- Improve my relationship with my husband, from finger pointing to hand holding

- Lose the 15 pounds I had gained from binge eating

- Feel more grounded and confident, holding my head high and knowing I can handle anything with grace and courage

Why Sundays? Because it's the beginning of the week. It sets the tone, and why wouldn't we want to begin our week with a plan, ready to charge forward? Grounded. Settled. Such a better way to thrive than squeezing your eyes shut tight, praying the week will be kind to you.

"The Bullet Journal"

Standing at a wall of journals in a store, Alina spied a bullet journal and was curious. What was this leather-bound book, full of dots? *This looks daunting*, Alina thought as she thumbed through the book. *I have no idea how to use this. Every page has dots, making a grid.* With a shake of her head and a sigh of resignation, she placed the book back on the shelf and started to walk away. After a few steps, though, she paused and looked back. Squinting her eyes, she pondered, *How can a book full of dots truly help me? I don't get it. Plus, I have no time for this.* Turning her back on the wall of books, she continued out the door.

However, the idea of the journal stayed with her.

In her life, she felt down-and-out. She was working in an underwhelming job that left her with few career opportunities and stuck in an environment she hated! However, the possibilities for changing careers felt mind-boggling, so she continued to fritter away her time and energy. She felt aimless and knew she needed to find a way out.

That bullet journal stuck in her memory, following her as she drudged her way through the day. Through research on Instagram, she learned how to use the journal; the creativity of the videos and posts grabbed her interest. She added it to her Christmas wish list. On that festive morning, under the magical white lights of her tree, wrapped in metallic paper was Alina's Christmas wish come true. Holding back her excitement, she decided New Year's Day would mark the beginning of her journaling path.

With coloured markers in hand, each week she made her way through the journal, decorating the pages to spark her creativity, keeping track of her moods, habits, to-do's, goals, and dreams. She customized her pages using glitter pens and metallic ink to add her own flair and flourish. Her imagination took hold as she designed her monthly calendars, adding quotes that spoke to her heart.

She relished the feeling of accomplishment as she marked her to-do's as completed—sometimes with a star or a heart. And with that feeling, she started to see herself as more grounded, centred, and intentional in the planning of her days. No longer aimless, now she felt methodical.

Midway through her first bullet journal year, she challenged herself to connect with professionals in fields that interested her, simply to ask, "May I interview you, to find out the steps you took in your career path?" Surprisingly, she received encouragement and mentorship through these interviews.

Alina told me, "The journaling process created a self-reflection tool that also sparked my imagination. I felt inner peace from the creative process, and more open to opportunities. I started to see possibilities and felt braver to seek out challenges."

A new career path emerged in a place where she felt joy and community, and her journaling process has become a lifelong habit of living intentionally.

The planning process—whether it's words on a page or beautiful drawings and design—becomes documentation of your reinvention. It is a keepsake of memories—some beautiful and some challenging—that displays the growth we all experience. Once the last page of the journal is filled, keep it! Hang on to your work as a memento of your journey. Looking back, you will see how you have evolved and moved forward with your life.

NOTEBOOK TIME: YOUR TO-DO'S

Start your own Sunday Planning Session.

1 First, choose a notebook that inspires you.
It should be one that brings joy and excitement into your life. Oh, planners, how I love you. The smell of the crisp papers! I grew up in the Mead notebook era of the 1980s. We've come a long way! The simplicity of a Moleskine is divine, or you can be "extra" like me, and choose a pastel, trendy notebook etched with a bold motto (*Conquer the World!* or *Never Stop Exploring!*). Bonus points: Choose a pen that inspires you! A Bic pen feels too pedestrian!

2 Find a quiet, distraction-free spot.
I love working at my kitchen table as the sunlight streams through the patio doors. I find I am most productive with the view of the huge maple tree.

Find a spot that feels good for you—a place where you feel inspired and creative. If you are having difficulty finding that spot, create one! Tidy up an area of your home; it doesn't need to be a large space.

Create comfort. I'm all about feeling cozy and comfortable when I am in creation mode. Make yourself a tea, a hot chocolate, or your favourite coffee. Light a candle—anything that makes you feel warm and nurtured as you write down every thought in your head.

3 With pen in hand, start writing!
This is a total brain dump. In this case, you're removing all the to-do's from your brain and putting them on the page. Randomly emptying your mind and transferring your thoughts onto paper is a way to bring a sense of peace.

4 **Organize your brainstorm (or brain dump).**
Now that you have everything set down on the page, analyze
and set your priorities. Some actions will take more than a week
to complete (most likely they can be broken down into smaller
steps). I love making little boxes beside my list to check off during
the week. Place deadlines and due dates on them to light a "get
it done" fire. Some of us, myself included, need self-imposed
deadlines or else work will endlessly drag on and never arrive at
completion.

5 **Once done, enjoy the rest of your day with the feeling of having accomplished your Sunday Planning Session.**
Everything you need to complete is out of your brain and onto
paper, so now you can have a restful Sunday.

6 **Throughout the week, review the Sunday Planning Session list
and get to work on those to-do's.**
This will help you stay on track and maintain focus. Granted, some
items will be amended (the four workout sessions may be edited
to three!), and some items will be carried over to the following
week—that's totally cool! When this happens, grant yourself some
grace instead of berating yourself. Nothing productive comes of
beating ourselves up.

Not sure what to write about in your Sunday Planning Session?
Here are some ideas to help guide you:

- Last week, what worked for me?
- Last week, what would I change?
- This week, what or how do I want to feel?
- Track your little wins.
- This made me smile…
- How many times will I move my body in the coming week?

- I dare myself to...
- I am capable of...
- This week, what will my self-care moments be?
- I will do less of...
- What am I grateful for?
- I will get this done...

Don't judge (especially your handwriting!). These are your thoughts, hopes, and dreams that you are putting on paper as they flow from your mind, down your arm, and through your fingers. They are how you feel inside, and if you start judging them, you will hold yourself back from making changes in your life.

12

YOUR ENVIRONMENT SHAPES YOU, SO MAKE IT GLAM!

"HOME!" SQUEALED the three-year-old toddler, sitting in his car seat as my car pulled up our driveway. The year was 2003. After a long day of caring for a class of 10 toddlers and picking up Matthew from daycare, my exhausted body couldn't wait to settle in for the evening. Although I was happy to be home, a feeling of dread started to sink in. The state of my house didn't make it feel like a haven—more like a reminder of unfinished projects and broken promises. My garden was a bed of overgrown weeds, with little flowers struggling to poke through for sunshine. Each time I saw my garden, I would remind myself, *All you gotta do is pull those damn weeds!* Instead, I would walk on.

Scratches and dents covered our weathered front door; the damn door handle kept breaking. With my head hung low, I stared at the dirty mat, questioning how I was ever going to make this dump of a house into my palace, a place I was proud to call home and where I was not ashamed to invite people over to enjoy my hospitality.

I regretted purchasing this house. For the economic climate of 2002, the deal was too good to pass up. We desperately wanted to enter the world of home ownership and Matthew's birth expedited our search. For years we had rented a beautiful lakefront apartment, with the sound of waves and ducks greeting us every morning. Our evenings were spent peacefully pushing the stroller along the pier while we savoured our ice cream cones. That was our idyllic existence as we dreamed about our future as a family.

"Hey! Let's buy a house!" I exclaimed to Mike during one of our evening strolls.

So the hunt began. We quickly found a previous rental turned sale—a three-bedroom townhouse that had been sitting on the market for six months and with a motivated seller. We negotiated $15,000 off the requested price—what a steal!

"It's a fixer-upper!" we told our families as we popped the champagne to celebrate our first major purchase.

The term "fixer-upper" was generous. The front door didn't close properly. There was no air conditioning. Stains on the carpet overlapped with one another. Multiple layers of wallpaper lined the walls, with some layers painted over instead of removed. The previous owner loved the show *Trading Spaces* (a popular TLC home improvement show that focused on DIY inspiration like gluing straw on the walls for a—cough— "dramatic effect") and the kitchen cupboards were heavily stencilled with pink-and-turquoise triangles and squares.

Two months into our home ownership, we discovered a mouse infestation and evidence of long-term habitation.

This house was not a steal. It was a category five disaster.

The excitement of new home ownership evaporated into a lump of buyers' remorse as the realization hit of the required hard work to improve our surroundings. I dove into a state of denial. We were stuck, doomed to live in a shitty home.

One day, while chilling out at Starbucks (by now you must have noticed my love of coffee shops), I overheard two friends as they huddled over a stack of home deco magazines. With their lattes and editions of *House Beautiful*, the young women were drawing up lists of home furnishing ideas.

"I just love my house. And these candle sets would look amazing in the living room!" one of the friends exclaimed as she earmarked a page in the magazine.

"That colour would look great in my kitchen," said the other, drawing a big circle around an image.

Instantly, I felt jealous that they got to have beautiful homes. I imagined their homes with grand staircases, chandeliers, fully decked-out kitchens with state-of-the-art appliances, and perfect clutter-free rooms. *Those lucky bitches, I bet they even have two-car garages!* Fate was smiling down on them with the award of star-worthy homes, while I quietly hated their existence.

And then I heard, "I know it's a small townhouse—we're sharing a bathroom and the basement is unfinished..."

Whaaaat?? Not a mansion? A townhouse like mine?

She went on, "But it belongs to me—I'm going to love and care for it."

Facepalm.

I realized that I'd never claimed my house. I still saw it as the ole rental unit that was treated like garbage. I purchased the previous owner's disaster and just carried on the legacy of neglect. I never decided to make the house my own and create an environment to thrive in. We were merely surviving—and I was waiting for "the next house" in order to feel at peace.

It was time to stop waiting.

The first step began with a dumpster in our driveway. A clean slate was needed, which meant a strict and brutal decluttering. We had accumulated years of "stuff" that was broken, and our way of dealing with it had been to move it to our garage. Out of sight, out of mind. But it was still psychologically weighing us down. The mountain of broken objects made it embarrassing to open my garage door and show the world proof of my chaotic existence. Not anymore.

Then, section by section and room by room, staying as emotionally neutral as possible, we sorted and forced ourselves to declutter. Renovations began with the kitchen, then the bathroom, and lastly the basement. With each renovation we claimed our space and designed a home to fuel us. Goodbye, broken children's toys. See you later, clothing from the 1990s. Adios, college textbooks and high school mementoes.

We yanked away the weeds and dead bushes in the front yard, and then it was time to replace the front door with a beautiful white steel door with a decorative glass insert.

A clearer path towards feeling at peace.

We started to feel lighter.

Happier.

Calmer.

Now, please don't read this and think that this all happened in one weekend. It didn't. The decluttering began and was completed due to our brutal honesty about stuff. The renovations occurred over a few years. As we took ownership of the space, we released our feelings of dread and failure—and started to feel the pride of ownership. Our little home, once considered a disaster, is now a home of dreams. It is a place where we feel capable, rejuvenated, self-reliant, and open to hosting visitors.

Recover Your Space

The environment where we spend the most time shapes our perspective and feelings. When we're living in a space that is cluttered and uninviting, we feel uninspired; that energy drags us down. Hard. Every time we enter this location, it affects our energy, and we carry the weight around with us all the time.

The mess.

The clutter.

The piles of stuff.

We see it, and in a moment we say to ourselves, *Ugh . . . I gotta deal with it.* Instead, we put the blinders on as protection for our psyche. However, deep down, the erosion begins.

It bugs.

It nags.

It sits in the back of our mind.

When we live in a cluttered environment, we are stuck in a state of overwhelm and broken promises. We lose to self-defeating thoughts because everywhere we look, we see proof of our lack of completion.

In order to overcome, we have to reclaim our space.

To do so requires us to deal with our mess.

To clean up the mess that we have created, we must put in the work and reset our domain. We are deserving of beautiful spaces that honour our soul and help us restore.

Now, I am not saying you have to have a mansion. Believe me, small-space living is possible. I am saying that you are deserving of an appealing environment that fills you up. At the end of a long day, you want a place that welcomes you with a big embrace, instantly leaving you feeling peaceful, calm, and revitalized.

Let's begin—here we go:

Action brings all these dreamy spaces to life. Start the process of reclaiming your space and get to work. Roll up those sleeves, get dirty, and purge in order to re-create those inspiring environments. Here is where our sense of personal responsibility comes to the fore as those old stacks of paper are jettisoned. Now get two bins—one for donations and one for garbage. Start in one area of your home, be brutal, and kick that stuff out of your life! Ditch! Ditch! Ditch! The kitschy ceramic lamb that you received at your eighth birthday party—do you still need it? The overflowing basket of unpaired socks that you forage through every morning, which leaves you wearing mismatched socks because you are running out of time—either hunker down and match them up, make some sock puppets, or purge them. (I recommend grabbing a glass of wine, putting on an episode of *Sex and the City*, and starting to pair them up. It's time to wear matching socks again.)

That box of *Teen Beat* magazines which brings back memories of awkwardness, big bangs, and over-teased hair—it's time to donate them so someone can cut them up to make crafts. Or, if you think they're collectible, sell them on eBay or Craigslist. (Just to be clear: these examples may or may not be items I decluttered from my home.)

By dealing with our clutter, we give ourselves room to breathe and create space for our mind to rest. As an added bonus, we are proving to ourselves that we are responsible— and that, my friend, is one of the best feelings in the world. The feeling that we are in control of our life. Once we take control of our environments—home, work, and even the car!— by reducing clutter and creating places for inspiration, we start to feel better about ourselves and our life.

Be warned: feelings of panic and overwhelm may appear. Please know it is normal to feel this way. We are focusing on progress, not perfection. A little step at a time, one square foot at a time. You can't change an entire house in one day (just like Rome wasn't built in a day), but each piece of effort will lead on to the next, and soon you will realize that you did it! You reclaimed your space.

Need help?

- Ask a friend.

- Hire an organizing professional.

- Make it a family project.

- Investigate online decluttering courses on Udemy and Skill-share, such as "30 Days to Declutter Bliss: How to Declutter Your World" and "Decluttering: Quickly Organize & Declutter Your Home."

Friendship Can Propel You Forward

Jennifer was a single parent of an eight-year-old son. Having survived a brutal marital separation, she was mourning the loss of her relationship and struggling with facing her new path. *My life wasn't supposed to be this way*, she told herself as she sank deeper into depression. Every day felt like a question of survival, and it took every ounce of her strength to get her son out to school and herself to work. Emotionally exhausted, her after-work routine involved binge-watching *The Office* and chilling out with a glass of wine. As she sat on the couch, physical reminders of her past—pictures on the walls, piles of unopened mail in the corner—surrounded her, adding to her downward spiral.

Moving wasn't an option. Her son was struggling with the divorce and she wanted to keep some consistency in his life; selling and moving him out of his home would have compounded the devastation he was feeling. However, she needed some kind of change to help her move forward, to release the past and open her arms towards the future. Changing her home environment on her own was too overwhelming for her. The feeling of "I have to do this by myself" was proof she was alone, and it made her feel isolated.

One evening, while endlessly scrolling through Netflix, the idea popped into her head to reach out to her girlfriends for help. Opening her phone, she typed out a group text to her friends:

Hey. I need help. In my house, everywhere I look is a reminder of the life I had. And I am sitting here—staring at this failure and disappointment. It's slowly killing me. I don't have the strength to do this myself—would someone be willing to come over, hold my hand and a box, while I purge this house? Kleenex will be needed.

Within minutes, her phone started to blow up.
"Hell yeah—this weekend works for me."
"Let's do it! I'm available."
"Purge! Purge! Purge!"
"I love to purge!"
"We'll make it a Purge-fest Party—girl style! I'll bring some food and drinks!"

And in one weekend, with the help of her friends, Jennifer successfully purged and decluttered every ounce of her home. A wave of relief washed over her as she started to dream again.

Her Wall Was Filled with Stilettos

Hanging neatly from a rack, RockerPoleChick's wall was filled with shoes. Sparkly ones. Neon colours. Metallic black. Five-inch heels. Even ones that glowed in the dark.

As I watched the pole challenge video on Instagram, my attention instantly turned to the magnificent display of glamorous shoes.

Lovers of Instagram know that it's a great platform for sharing workouts, especially pole moves; it's a hotbed for challenges. For the month of June, I cohosted a Pole Basics challenge with Studioveena and GisellePoleArt. As you may recall from chapter four, Julie Brand (also known as Veena) created Studioveena.com, a website where anyone can learn to pole at home. GisellePoleArt is a pole dancer in Switzerland who posts her work on Instagram. Working on a list of 10 pole moves, pole dancing enthusiasts shared their videos to their accounts, and we cheered them on. It was a great way for people to stay accountable to their training and create community.

As I perused everyone's video submissions, I was able to virtually peek into their pole rooms. A pole room is a space for your pole, where you can practise and dance. Some folks have a whole room dedicated to their practice, while others find a little corner in their basement, rec room, or bedroom. Everyone decorated their pole space in a way that reflected their own personality and style. Feather boas! Curtain lights! Motivational sayings on the walls and wavy mirrors!

And then there was RockerPoleChick's awesome wall of shoes.

"OMG I love your space!" I enthusiastically direct-messaged her.

She texted back, "On tough days, I enter this room, shut the door behind me, and turn on my favourite songs. For an hour, I slink across the floor, dance around the pole, test my strength, and work on my moves. The stress of the day fades away and I feel new again."

Whether it is a pole room or a glamorous space, we all need a place where we allow our hard moments to fade away.

NOTEBOOK TIME: YOUR TO-DO'S

Write about spaces that fuel you (and then create them!).

It's time to explore the spaces that we spend the most time in, and analyze them. Ask yourself, How do I want to feel in this space? It can be your home, office, basement—even your car. Write in your notebook how you want to feel in those spaces.

- Inspired?
- Rested?
- Energized?
- Nurtured?
- Romantic?
- Decadent?
- Elegant?

Create these feelings using colours, textures, and objects (but don't clutter back up!). Explore design and home magazines to see what environments reflect your feelings. Look for inspiration when you are out and about—in a restaurant, hotel, gallery, or museum. Take a picture of a space that you would like to re-create in your home.

Start dreaming of a space that brings you joy.

Don't forget to add a special place in your home for inspiration. This might be a cozy spot where you can curl up with a cup of tea, or it might even be a romantic bedroom. You can even create a shelf of inspiration—where you display pictures and objects that leave you feeling energized when you look at them. One of my students has a board on her wall where she adds pictures, words, and notes of inspiration.

These reminders will influence and motivate you.

Once you have written about your ideal spaces and how you want to feel in them, it's time for action. Start re-creating those settings to feed your energy with positivity and give yourself a place to feel refreshed. It comes down to a matter of choice—choosing to live in a place that drags you down or in one that lifts you up.

With effort and dedication, we can reinvent our locations, elevating our confidence and self-esteem in the process. We come to recognize that we are worthy of a clean, organized, and beautiful space, regardless of the square footage of our home or its location in our neighbourhood.

While I was writing this chapter, my home became cleaner and I created a special spot in my backyard with an outdoor couch placed under our maple tree.

Sipping a glass of Prosecco, I dream as I stare up at the leaves rustling in the wind. The birds chirp, the wind blows, and I lose all sense of time.

If you are looking for me, that's where you'll find me.

13

THE STUMBLING BLOCKS TO FEELING SEXY

O N DECEMBER 21, 2005, the Supreme Court of Canada made a groundbreaking ruling on consensual group sex and swinger activities. In the highest-level court case *Jean-Paul Labaye v. Her Majesty the Queen*, Jean-Paul Labaye was charged with operating a "common bawdy house," a violation under section 210(1) of the Criminal Code, for owning the club L'Orage, where people who paid the membership fees could assemble and engage in consensual group sex. This ruling protected such venues from the threat of police intervention, resulting in more private establishments springing up (pardon the pun) throughout Canada, especially in metropolitan areas such as Toronto and Vancouver. My connections from owning a pole dancing studio and performing in burlesque shows led me to teaching pole dancing at a swingers club named Oasis Aqualounge, once a month for a year.

One Friday a month, I would venture 40 minutes out of my suburban world to Toronto, to teach pole dancing at Oasis, a water-themed adult playground located in a beautifully restored 19th-century mansion. Spanning four floors, this clothing-optional environment included two bars and dance floors, an indoor hot tub, a year-round outdoor heated pool in a private courtyard, and "play rooms" on the top floor. (*Ding! Ding!* You're correct if you are wondering if the play rooms were for sex.) With an upscale, sophisticated decor, Oasis was known as a sex-positive, non-judgmental place where there was nothing sexier than consent. (A strict "ask once" policy was in effect to cut down harassment and unwanted touching. Anyone who broke that rule had to leave the premises.)

The emphasis on creating a no-pressure, carefree environment was essential. If someone wanted to walk around naked—wonderful, feel free! Here's a locker to place your valuables and here's a towel to place between your bottom and chairs. Want to keep your clothes on? Fabulous! This is a place where people of all genders and sexualities can play with their partners and feel liberated. You might be asking yourself, Who visits a swingers club? Well, my friend, it's doctors, teachers, dentists, students, people working in retail, young folks, older folks. Married. In a relationship. People who are looking to spice up their world. You guessed it—everyday people. (I may or may not have seen my old college professor with her husband... shhhhh!)

My role, as resident pole instructor, wearing my tank top and booty shorts, was to teach pole moves on the club's main floor as a form of entertainment and fun for the couples. By offering a fun lesson in pole, I welcomed the club members, helping them "break the ice"—to feel more at ease. While I was paid by the club, I was also allowed to promote my business.

(Interestingly, I discovered that a lot of people from my suburb ventured to Oasis.)

At the end of the night, dressed in my favourite Red Sparkle Magic costume (a bra-and-bottom outfit covered—you guessed it—with red Swarovskis), I'd perform a pole routine, take my bow, and return home before the clock struck midnight, like a pole dancing Cinderella. I loved my Friday nights teaching pole at Oasis. (Fun fact: on top of being paid to pole, I could choose between paid parking and fuel or a free glass of bubbly. Turning down champagne is sacrilege, but my practical side always won out.)

One Friday night, as I was finishing up a lesson, a couple stood off to the side, waiting for a turn. They looked like complete opposites. She was short with an ample body, and her partner was a tall and skinny fella. She was naked. He was wearing black leather pants, a chain-link vest, and a top hat.

"I heard someone is teaching pole. Can I have a turn?" she asked.

"Yes ma'am. I'm Jane!" I replied, reaching out my hand.

"I'm Lisa and this is my husband, Mark. I like to be naked—it's kinda part of my thing. Will that make you uncomfortable?"

I smiled reassuringly. "Not at all. I'm teaching pole lessons in a sex club—nothing phases me." A memory of the early "vulgar woman shaming incident" experience flashed through my mind, leading me to realize how much more at ease I'd become with sharing my love of pole.

In her lesson, I taught her how to walk around the pole, flip her hair, push out her hip for a booty accent. Every move I taught was fun and easy to do and made her feel sexy. There was nothing difficult, only moves that prompted giggles and flirtiness.

At the end of the lesson, I asked Lisa why she and her husband visited Oasis. What attracted her to these environments?

"We live in Michigan. I work in human resources and my husband is an accountant. Every six months we drop off our kids with my parents and cross the border, driving to Toronto. This is our sexy-weekend time. I look forward to this time, away from responsibilities. Look, I know my body is bigger. I've had a lot of babies. But I feel comfortable in my body here. I am naked the whole weekend. Mark likes to dress as a rocker. In this place, I feel beautiful and sexy. I don't care how my body looks because everyone here doesn't care. I feel accepted. Then we go home and I'm energized. No one knows I do this. My parents just think we're visiting museums, restaurants, and the CN Tower. It's my secret weekend."

By having an adventure and stepping out of her comfort zone, she felt more courageous. As well, being in an environment of different body types where everyone felt free and comfortable allowed her to accept her own body more easily— cellulite and wiggly bits and all!

Seeing other people's bodies—up close and personal—led her to understand that the media's portrayal of beauty doesn't reflect real life. We all have our folds, dimples, jiggles, and flabby bits of flesh. Releasing the body shame helped break down the stumbling blocks to feeling sexy.

For Lisa, her personal stumbling blocks were not having enough time (a busy working parent of school-aged children) and not feeling comfortable with her body. She sidestepped the stumbling blocks by dedicating time away from her busy life so she could feel more relaxed, and by surrounding herself with people who celebrate body diversity. When you're encircled by people who see beauty in people's skin, you start to infuse this spirit of self-love into your soul.

Is the Word "Sexy" a Stumbling Block?

Placing her 10-pound weights on the shelf, my private-lesson client Christine, a 42-year-old lawyer, revealed to me, "To be honest, when I hear the word 'sexy,' I think powerless. I get my back up."

"Oh, why is that?" I questioned.

"I see it as a sign of weakness—that instead of using your brain and intelligence, you use your body. 'Sexy' is a weak word, in my opinion."

"Interesting. What if the word was 'sass' or 'bold'?" I offered.

A smile lit up Christine's face. "Oh! I like those words. Being bold and having sass feels freeing to me."

"All right, so change your definition of 'sexy' to one that feels more reflective of how you feel."

A week later, during our private lesson, Christine shared with me, "I'm loving feeling bold and having sass. I swear, I am carrying myself better. I think I've even started to strut!"

To be honest with you, prior to deep-diving into the world of pole, I would have agreed with Christine. Being in my forties, the women I had viewed as sex symbols when I was growing up were people like Suzanne Somers, Bo Derek, and Farrah Fawcett, who were celebrated less for their intelligence and more for their physical "assets." Their popularity hinged not on their brains but on beauty and bust size. In *Selves, Symbols, and Sexualities: An Interactionist Anthology*, Thomas S. Weinberg and Staci D. Newmahr concur: from the 1950s through to the 1980s, despite women's growing political and economic power, their desirability resided less in what they could do in the world and more in their aesthetics. Think of it—can you recall a media reference to a sex symbol's SAT scores or how well they did in school? However, you can easily find their body measurements.

Like Christine, growing up, the message I received was that the busty bombshell persona had to hide her intellect, so I too felt disgust with the word "sexy." After spending years helping people slink, slide, and flow around a pole, though, I've come to the realization that you can embrace the carefree feeling of sexy and still be smart at the same time. You aren't leaving any part of you behind.

Perhaps "sexy" is an overused word? A vague description that garners either a positive response or a look of indignation? You can soften the response by opening up the definition and exploring other synonyms, creating your own version, an interpretation that feels more harmonious with your nature. Consider words like *bodacious, hot, energized, inspired, sensuous, sassy, alluring, naughty, sizzling, ravishing, infatuating, blissful, captivating, enthralling, magical, mystical, evocative, sleek, silky, delicious, provocative, fascinating, compelling, enticing.*

My favourite is "mesmerizing." I love how it sounds when I say it. "Mezzz-merize"—so yummy! Damn, so fabulous!

The definition is purely individual. We all have our own ideas based on our experiences. It's subjective. For you, the word could produce a feeling, a result, or an action. It could be something you wear that ignites your spirit. (Or do you feel sexy and then it shows in what you wear? This feels like a chicken-and-egg scenario!) Explore your definition. Is it a feeling? Or an action that creates a feeling? Am I confusing you? This was the big discussion one night in the studio: does the feeling of sexy come from inside or outside?

Merriam-Webster's definition of "sexy" lends itself to an external interpretation: "she had sexy eyes," "her legs were long and sexy." But I can tell you, if I don't feel sexy on the inside, it doesn't matter if I am wearing Agent Provocateur with kick-ass hair, flawless makeup complete with lashes, and killer Pleaser heels. I don't feel sexy if, deep down, I experience myself as gross and bloated—like putting on a corset after feasting on all-you-can-eat sushi. Barf. Then I'm definitely not mesmerizing!

However, again, it can be the other way around. You may not be "feeling it," wearing your hoodie and jeans and feeling like total shit, but then put on a flattering dress that curves your shape and create killer eye makeup and you feel like a million bucks! Look out, world!

Heather, 52 years old, shared with me, "There's this pair of black boots that I have owned for years. And whenever I wear them, I feel powerful. Like a superhero."

When we feel sexy, it's because we have taken care of both our body and our emotions; we have prioritized self-care. That means healthy eating, getting enough rest, and building up our confidence as a way to generate energy that fuels us. Self-care happens when we place our needs for rest and relaxation on our "to-do" list instead of leaving it up to chance. Let's face it, you may have enjoyed it when you ate pizza and wings or stayed up late, or when you sat around watching *The Office* all day, but to call those things "feeling bold" is a mighty stretch.

To *be* or *feel* sexy, bold, or sassy, you don't need to have a "model-perfect" body. Let's take a look at Jacki's story...

Creating Confidence

As Jacki's eyes scanned the image on her laptop, her heart started to beat faster. Her screen displayed a JPEG of herself on all fours, wearing a black bra, panties, and black fishnets with oversized diamonds. Her long, wavy dark hair with hints of red was draped over the side of her face, slightly covering her eye. With a come-hither look, her slight smile enticed the camera. She remembered that when the boudoir photographer suggested she position her hands and knees on the soft grey blanket, she felt a swirl of "Holy shit, what am I doing?" excitement.

Gazing with admiration at her photo, staring at her face and hair, her eyes trailed down her body.

"Oh, love this," she grinned, marvelling at the fierceness in her eyes. "Hair on point. Thank heavens for my stylist. Loving my nails."

As her vision approached her stomach, though, Jacki caught her breath. "Oh jeez."

There it was. A sagging tummy. Gravity pulling her loose, stretch-marked epidermis towards the ground.

During the photo shoot, her third, she felt so free and fierce, the most confident and the sexiest she had ever felt. Over the years, she had participated in boudoir photo shoots as a way of expressing her sexuality. Her first shoot was awkward and unsettled. Her body felt stiff and her self-confidence was shredded after her divorce from her spouse, who would tell her, "You're cute but not beautiful." Although she felt clumsy during the photography experience, she was intrigued by being seen as sexy.

Between her first and second shoots, she experienced major changes in her sexuality. No longer limiting herself to hetero-sexuality, she explored polyamory and pansexuality. Formerly needing to be convinced she was sexy, now she knew it. Her second photo shoot, in a dilapidated barn, in which she wore a laced-up bustier, lace panties, and thigh-high stockings, high-lighted her evolution. She enjoyed the relaxed vibe. She felt much sexier.

And now, on the screen, in her third photo shoot—the expe-rience in which she felt the sauciest and most playful—she could see her belly drooping over her panties.

"To hell with this. This is my body. I am the whole package."
And opening up another tab on her laptop screen, she turned to a private Facebook group—Lush & Lace and Boudoir Babes, a community she enjoyed—and shared her image with a special caption: "This belly represents babies, happiness, ice cream, and cheesecake. It's a revolutionary act to love yourself as you are."

With the cursor hovering over Post, Jacki exhaled and launched her Facebook update.

Kimberly, another friend of mine, had her life shattered by a marital breakup that left her hopes and dreams in ruins. "It was grief that made life unbearable and sucked my joy." At 38 years old, she was devastated and angry, furious that her dreams had been stolen from her. She was livid at the thought of having to "start my life over again."

And the thought of feeling sexy made her want to vomit.

The dark cloud followed her wherever she went, especially when she attended parties with her friends. The vibe she was putting out was "Be careful, I will shred you apart."

To recover, she needed to detox from the hell. With the support of a therapist, she examined her feelings and slowly rediscovered her identity and started along a new path.

IN ALL these stories I have shared with you, there is one common theme. These people all overcame personal difficulties and created swagger—that quality people have when they behave with confidence, knowing they have value and worth. Because they know who they are and where they want to go in life, there's a strut and poise about each and every one of them. This is what I wish for you to have—a confidence born from empowerment to make your own decisions and be comfortable in your body.

NOTEBOOK TIME: YOUR TO-DO'S

In your notebook, write your thoughts about the following questions:

- How do you feel when you see the word "sexy"?

- Is there a synonym that leaps out for you?

- What do you think are your stumbling blocks as you seek to feel this way? Energy? Time? Or is it how you feel about your body?

14

BOLDLY BE YOU

THE GIANT martini glass dazzled under the lights, covered from top to bottom with 150,000 glistening Swarovski crystals. Star-struck (yes, by an inanimate object), I stood at the edge of the stage at the Phoenix Concert Theatre in Toronto. Known as the "Swarovski Martini," this iconic, massive art deco–style stage prop was created for Dita Von Teese, the legendary burlesque star, who would swish and swirl around inside it as part of her famous neo-burlesque act, stirring audiences all the way from the Crazy Horse in Paris, France, to the Roxy Theatre on the Sunset Strip in Los Angeles. Classically trained in ballet, she re-popularized the burlesque scene, earning the moniker "Queen of Burlesque."

Pinching myself, I couldn't believe my luck. I was getting to perform in *Dita Von Teese Live*, her first-ever show in Toronto. Miss Mitzy Cream, whom I performed with in many shows, was coproducing this spectacle, meticulously hiring performers for this "variety show–style" event. When I heard about her search for a pole act, I fiercely shouted, "Me! Me! Me!" and made it past the "performer velvet rope" into the VIP section of this epic burlesque adventure!

For five years, I had been performing in the Toronto burlesque scene, gaining a reputation for crowd-pleasing acrobatic performances, all in beautifully crafted costumes by Manuge et Toi, Canada's number one burlesque costume designer. Being a dynamic pole performer, I brought variety to shows, setting myself apart from other acts. If every performer is the same, boredom overcomes the audience and they start playing with their phones. (Believe it or not, witnessing the same way of taking off clothing can become repetitious and dull.)

In addition, I had a reputation for being easy to work with, showing up on time and never frustrating the show producer or manager. I was quick to respond, emailing my technical stage requirements sheets without being asked twice. Show producers crave this kind of performer. I was responsible for my free-standing stage pole from set-up to take-down (another of my ninja skills—I could build a pole stage in less than two minutes flat). Having a reputation for being easy-peasy to work with is important; you might be a scintillating superstar onstage, but a backstage "Dilemma Diva from Hell" will never be booked again by any show producer.

Arriving three hours early for my technical rehearsal, I entered a quiet theatre populated only by the lighting, stage, and sound crews, preparing for the evening's extravaganza. *Wahoo! First performer arrived!* I told myself with pride.

From my years of experience, I know that my performance onstage is directly affected by my preparation and pre-show rituals. I love arriving early, to savour the stillness of the theatre, cherish the rising anticipation of the show, and dedicate myself to a thorough physical warm-up (because this body struggles with flexibility). I loved staring at the empty stage, envisioning my performance and feeling the movement in my body.

As I made my way across the floor of the theatre towards the stage for my pre-show "envisioning" ritual, I noticed the gorgeous four-foot-tall martini glass inhabiting the space. It was glorious. As I studied the pattern of the crystals, time stood still.

"It's beautiful, isn't it?" a soft-spoken voice danced behind me, breaking my trance.

"Oh my god, it's magnificent. Hey, does this mean that Dita is here?" I wondered aloud, turning towards the voice.

Standing before me with that perfectly coiffed raven hair wrapped in a lilac-coloured scarf and those bright-red lips, porcelain skin, and signature beauty mark—

The Queen.

Dita. Von. Teese.

The air escaped my lungs. "You're here!" I inhaled.

Reaching out her deep-red nail-polished hand, she said, "Yes, I'm Dita, pleased to meet you. And you are?"

I swear, I almost curtsied. Part of me questioned whether I should drop to my knees, like Wayne and Garth of *Wayne's World*, and proclaim, "I'm not worthy! I'm not worthy!" Instead, I shook her hand and stammered, "I'm Jane... er... I mean... I'm 'Natalia Rose'... I mean, I'm really Jane, but my stage name is Natalia Rose. I'm so honoured to be in your show."

Ugh. Facepalm. Total "burlesque rookie" fail.

"Nice to meet you, Natalia Rose," she giggled. "How long have you been performing in burlesque?"

Blushing, I admitted, "Fairly new to burlesque. About five years, and mostly in the Toronto area. I hear this show is going to be packed. Is it true?"

Her eyes lit up. "Oh yes. We're almost sold out." (Although we were standing in an empty hall at that moment, the Phoenix Concert Theatre has a capacity of 1,350 people.)

Goosebumps instantly spread across my arms, with a touch of anxious nausea in my stomach. "Oh dear god, that's the biggest audience I have ever performed in front of. Oh no." Suddenly, a wave of panic hit. I prayed I wouldn't forget my performance moves.

Seeing the sudden paleness in my face and my "deer in headlights" look, Dita touched my arm. "Artists who are unafraid and don't hold back grab the audience's attention. Be free. Relax. The audience is on your side, and they want you to do well, so remember—just be you. You'll be fine." She smiled, and softly walked backstage to greet newly arrived performers. Or should I say, she floated. The woman's feet seemed never to touch the floor! (Oh, and by the way... Dita Von Teese touched my arm! O.M.Gee.)

My performance opened the second half of the show, right after the intermission. Onstage, dressed in stunning ringmaster bustier attire, the raven-haired Laura Desiree, host of *Naked News* and headlining burlesque star, introduced me to the audience, my portable pole stage standing behind her as I waited in the wings. Deep-breathing to calm my nerves, I closed my eyes and remembered Dita's words: "Be free. Relax. The audience is on your side."

I was feeling butterflies in my stomach as I heard, "Friends of all genders..." I love it when I hear that phrase, because we *all* deserve to show up for this! I heard her as she continued, "Please welcome Natalia Rose to the stage!" A big smile spread across my face. It was showtime.

I entered the stage, looking up to the audience with a big smile and a nod. Arriving at my pole stage, wearing my silver booty shorts, a white mesh halter top, and a massive, ornate silver necklace (which was sewn into the mesh to hold it in place), I struck my starting pose, ready for "Don't Stop Me Now" by Queen to begin.

As Freddie Mercury's voice filled the concert hall, calling everyone to have themselves a real good time, my body instantly began the routine. The whole performance lasted three and a half minutes, and it felt like an out-of-body experience. Because I was well rehearsed, meaning the movements were memorized by my muscles, I could enjoy the moment with the audience. And what an audience. From the front of the stage to the back wall, it was like a sea of people! Crammed together, they screamed as I flew into multiple pull-ups on a spinning pole (similar to doing a chin-up but spinning round and round on the pole—total beast move). Landing my finishing pose, I held the position as the crowd roared with appreciation. *Hold. Don't break the pose; soak in the applause,* I reminded myself. Feeling the audience love, I slowly released the final hold and stepped out to take my bow.

As I exited the stage to the wings, I was greeted by the stagehands, congratulating me for an excellent performance. I looked towards the back hallway, to Dita's open dressing room door. She stood there in her long black satin robe and gave me a sweet, approving wink. She was right: when you are free and relaxed, the audience truly has your back.

The Martini Glass Performance

But I would be remiss if I didn't share with you Dita's majestic martini glass performance. I witnessed it from the wings, alongside the stagehands. Truly regal, she elegantly mounted the steps to climb into the martini glass and swirled around in the water. Wearing a pink G-string and panties (both covered with Swarovskis, of course), she flirted with the audience, arching her back and flicking water with her pointed red-polished toes. The audience adored her. To end her performance, she curled up in the martini glass and leaned over the rim, waving her fingers to the audience.

After the curtain closed, one of the stagehands hustled up to her with a massive pink towel. Wrapping her up, the stagehand remarked, "Holy smokes, you're ice-cold!"

Dita sighed. "Yes, the water was freezing. We forgot to heat it up. It's okay, the audience couldn't tell."

THAT, my friend, is professionalism, and I will never forget her "un-Diva-ness."

"She's So Unusual"

When we feel confident, secure in our weirdness, we push the self-doubt monster to the curb and open up to new experiences and new people. Our self-image is strong; we feel awesome and are kinder to ourselves. We make eye contact with people, greet the cashier at the checkout with a "Hello! How are you?" (instead of keeping our faces in our phones), because we are ready to actively show up and engage with the world.

Speaking of embracing our freaky side—let's cut to Cyndi Lauper's *She's So Unusual* album of 1983. *Yes!* We're talking about a 38-year-old album, my friend, and for good reason: the album was a breakout success for Cyndi, who, prior to releasing it, suffered bankruptcy and was working in retail stores and singing in local clubs. For the album cover, she blasted out her New Wave persona and wore her vintage red prom-style dress that she purchased at her place of employment, Screaming Mimi's. Clad in fishnets and covered in heavy costume jewellery, Cyndi is photographed mid–dance pose on Henderson Walk in Coney Island. At the time it was released, the cover won a Grammy for Best Recording Package, and in 2019 the album was selected by the Library of Congress for preservation in the National Recording Registry for being "culturally, historically or aesthetically significant."

Can you imagine, after filing for bankruptcy, if Cyndi Lauper had chosen to turn down her New Wave volume and donned a button-up cotton polo shirt, khakis, and Keds— essentially, becoming *usual*? We would never have enjoyed "Time after Time," "Girls Just Want to Have Fun," and "All through the Night," and, later on, the musical *Kinky Boots*! She turned up the freakin' volume and got louder.

How do we regain confidence in our weird and wonderful selves when life has kicked us down? When our ego is bruised more than a banana left in our lunch bag and rejection has allowed the "self-doubt monster" to tear us apart? We embrace our inner Cyndi Lauper and choose to give it another shot. Just as Cyndi leaned into her uniqueness when she had every reason to doubt (and was rewarded with fame and success), we, too, can rebuild our self-confidence from the inside out.

NOTEBOOK TIME: YOUR TO-DO'S

1 Plan to invest in a coach or therapist.
If you are someone who suffers from anxiety (I raise my hand here), you need to be supported by a therapist or coach. Getting to the heart of the matter will slingshot you towards healing and renewal. Remove any shame you might feel about having a therapist; leaders and champions turn to coaches to maintain their goals and energy. Having a coach can be a game changer.

2 Try something new.
Sign up for opportunities to try new experiences and then follow through. (You know how I feel about bailing. Sign up and

show up!) Curious about a cooking class? Find a class—physical or online—sign up, and show up. Write a list of activities that grab your curiosity. Not feeling inspired? Carry around your notebook and whenever you hear of an experience that sounds interesting, write it down. Don't believe you have time? Actually, you do. Look at how you use your time. If you are spending your nights on the couch with endless Facebook scrolling (no judgment here—I've been sucked into that vortex many times), then you do have time. Take something off your plate in order to create space/time. Rearrange in order to create more time.

3   **Get comfortable with your weirdness.**
We all have something about ourselves that is unique. Perhaps a little weird. Growing up, we learn to hide our differences as a way to blend in and be accepted, to be a part of the group. The idea of being outside the group is scary and isolating, so we work overtime to be just like everyone else. We push aside our uniqueness in order to be accepted.

When we become comfortable with our weirdness, accepting what makes us strange and different from others, we celebrate and own it.

Make a list of what is unique about you. Rediscover your individuality.

4   **Increase your positive self-talk and decrease the negative words in your head.**
Can you imagine if we said to a child the words we say to ourselves? If they are horrible and soul-crushing, you wouldn't dare say them to a child! However, for some reason, we think it's okay to say them to ourselves.

Or how about this—if the words you say to yourself were broadcast for the world to hear? As though an imaginary speaker were attached to your brain, so everyone could hear you say, "I should have done better." "Oh, I suck at this." "Damn it, why am I even bothering?" Trust me, someone would intervene. Someone would stop and say, "Hey, that's enough. I'm your cheerleader and I can see how special you are."

Well, consider this an intervention. It's time to stop cutting ourselves down. When we mentally rip ourselves apart, it shows in how we carry ourselves and in our appearance. It may even show up in how we treat other people. The words we feed to our soul show up in our presence. So we're going to counteract this by filling our soul with personal kindness and soothing encouragement, and becoming a cheerleader—pompoms and all! No need to try out for this cheer team—you are the squad, because cheerleading is a way of life. A cheerleader is a role model, a leader, and a friend who jumps and dances the team into success, even building that cheer pyramid. It's time to fiercely propel your way to victory. Weird and wonderful acts of self-acceptance will go a long way, especially when you are doing your best!

Abraham Maslow, the American psychologist who created Maslow's Hierarchy of Needs, stated, "Each person, simply by being, is inherently worthy." (Oh! There's my former preschool teacher sneaking in.) The positive or negative actions and experiences that make up our past do not negate our worth and value. You, my friend, have faced ups and downs, victories and setbacks, throughout your life and will continue to do so in the future. Along your journey, you will always have merit and significance. No matter what. Shine bright, embrace your unusualness, and enter each room like a freakin' rock star!

CONCLUSION

BEFORE WE declare this meeting adjourned, let's review how far we have come. (I love looking back to see growth.) Grab your "Uniquely Me" notebook to brush up. We started this journey together drinking tea (or champagne) from my mother's vintage Rosenthal china. We realized that life wasn't always what we had thought it was going to be, and we explored how we might change our lives. We conquered our negative self-talk, busted our fears, and abandoned our FOMO Facebook-scrolling ways. We ceased the bingeing and escaping behaviours to face what was holding us back. Yes, sometimes we may retreat to watching cat videos, but we do not spiral back down into the abyss of procrastination.

Together, we released sad, pent-up emotions that were dragging us down, in order to transform a space in which to nourish and revive—a place to retreat from the day, and one that best reflects our individuality and offers calmness. By decluttering what no longer serves us, we opened our world to feel joy and freedom.

For many of us, we navigated our internal obstacles in order to try something new—whether it was organizing a photo shoot, joining a club, trying a new workout, or even spending a weekend naked in a sex club with a trusted and loving partner (and returning home feeling mischievous).

By discovering and embracing our weirdness, we now exude a relaxed vibe that attracts people into our lives who will love and encourage us. Being part of a revolution and a community is more enjoyable than venturing alone. Change is much easier when we have someone cheering us on, sharing our enthusiasm when we rack up our little wins and add to our "I'm a Rock Star" evidence file. We rise up, grow, and explore this new path together, because when one of us trips, the other can reach over and lend a hand.

Our lives are more complex than our parents' and grandparents', and that's okay.

Along with more opportunities come expectations and demands, which we can handle. We no longer allow our *Poor me* and *I could never do that* thoughts to make our decisions. We proclaim to the world that IT'S OUR TIME. If we stumble, we brush the dirt off our muscle tank top, pull our shoulders back, flex our biceps, and hold our head high.

And when someone calls us vulgar, we respond with, "Hell yeah, you bet we are!" We stand tall, with our shoulders back and wearing our cape to show we're the champion in our own story.

Being "up to no good" means we are strong, confident, and sexy and can handle any situation with grace and courage. As we learned from Layla Duvay, we never know when our time on this planet will be up, so let's live by our own design.

Wear those shorts that make your legs look long and allow your cheeks to peek through. Free your gluteal fold!

Put on your sparkly platform Pleaser heels, and while you dance, bang them on the floor to make a statement and steal attention. Or simply because you love the sound of a heel bang. It's a glorious sound!

Do a hair flip to bring you joy! And above all else, live by your own version of strength, sexiness, and confidence.

It has been a joy and an honour to share these stories of reinvention with you. Looking ahead to the future, my arms are wide open to the opportunities ahead, because I know full well that our resilience will always show. Reinvention continues.

And with a stiletto in hand as a gavel, I declare this meeting adjourned.

ACKNOWLEDGMENTS

WITHOUT THE LOVE and support of the pole dancing community, this book would never have existed. You entrusted me the responsibility to represent our love of pole, and I hope I honoured our world. Thank you for being the inspiration and foundation for the Up To No Good Club.

My gratitude to everyone I interviewed for the book. By sharing your story, you created a powerful opportunity for others to heal and feel inspired. I hold your experiences in high regard.

To my husband, Michael. For more than 25 years, it's been you and me against the world. The foundation of our lives is grounded in the spirit of "place your bets on us." I love our entrepreneurial zest, and I'm grateful for your love and support. Together, we created two smart, kind, and loving children, Matthew and Brendan. Thank you for loving me as I am.

Kristina Paider, thank you for the moment on Zoom when you leaned towards the camera and proclaimed, "Jane, yes! You are a writer. Your story needs to be read and I believe in you." Forever etched in my memory as a turning point to becoming an author. Thank you for seeing the writer in me and helping me shape what it's like to be up to no good. You are a gifted developmental editor. (Sidebar: you helped me curb my overuse of exclamation marks!!)

Shout-out to the Page Two team. Thanks to Jesse and Gabrielle, the ever-patient publishing project managers; Emily and John, my amazing editors; Taysia, for her patience as cover designer; and Meghan, for geeking out over online marketing with me. Nikkie Stinchcombe, you brought poise and style to the cover illustrations of The Up To No Good Ladies. Thank you for capturing their personality and style.

To my brother, Jason, and my father, Keith. If it wasn't for your financial gifts, my pole studio, connections, and friendships would never have been created. Your belief in my vision, as zany as it sounded, started me on my life-changing journey. My love and appreciation to Renate Mcintosh and Nancy Konzuk for being strong, fierce, and determined role models in my life. To Heather Poulin, from Girl Guides, youth group, high school, and now pole dancing, our friendship has lasted decades. You're not just a friend; you're a sister to me. Thank you for being you (cue the *Golden Girls* theme song).

Michelle Mynx and Kim Neal, it's difficult to put into words how much your friendship means to me—you're an extension of my family. You inspire me with your strength, resilience, advocacy, and love for each other.

Layla Duvay, you left an indelible mark on many people's lives. Your rock star sass will be forever remembered by bringing our Up To No Good Club to the world.

Jamie Waggoner, my fellow tap-dancing diva and "let's put on a show" partner in crime. Thank you for believing in me and cheering me on. Cathryn Haynes, your creative ability shaped the vision of my studio, and I enjoyed our years of working together. Moreover, your friendship has meant the world to me. Marissa Saunders, over the years, you've photographed the evolution of my pole life and now my transition to author. Your work reminds me of the beauty within all of us.

Chair Cabaret and Rock Bottom students—teaching our online classes brought connection and purpose to my lockdown life. I loved being up to no good with you, especially during a pandemic!

My heartfelt thanks to Chalene Johnson, Elisabeth Magalhaes, Ellen Latham, Ellie Parvin, Jen Stillion, Julie Brand, Katie Soy, Liane Davey, Marci Warhaft, Melissa Joy Olson, Natalie Borch, and Susan Sandler for navigating a pandemic to review this book. I am so grateful for your time and energy.

Double thanks to the following ladies: Chalene, thank you for being my mentor from afar. By sharing your knowledge, you helped me design the best life for my family. Elisabeth, thank you for the years of moral support, especially for answering the texts beginning with "Got a minute?" And Jen, your California sunshine brightens my life.

Finally, to every person who took a chance and walked through the doorway of my studio and played on the poles. From my heart, thank you. Your willingness to step out of your comfort zone inspired me and I will forever treasure our time, filled with hair tossing, dancing to "The Naughty List of Songs," and climbing to the top of the poles. Always remember: boldly be you.

ABOUT
THE AUTHOR

JANE WILSON has taught over 10,000 people to feel strong, sexy, and confident. As founder and former owner of PoleFit Nation, she spent over a decade teaching pole, fitness, heels, and striptease dance classes while encouraging women to flip their hair, bang their heels, and love their curves. She uses her Instagram accounts (@TheJaneWilson and @BeginnerPoleDancing) to encourage women to reclaim their spark. With her vivacious and honest manner, she shares how to make time for play and handle any obstacle with grace. She is a Canadian Pole Fitness Masters Champion and has been featured in *Canadian Living* and on *Cityline*.

HI THERE, IT'S JANE!

I hope you're feeling inspired to create your own Up To No Good Club!

Want to know one of the secrets behind the success of my pole dancing studio? Reviews.

For over a decade, I had a monthly habit of requesting testimonials from clients. Whether it was a recent bachelorette party or a new or super-dedicated student, I put my fear of rejection aside and asked for a review. Oh, the breakout of cold sweat!

Now, with a deep breath, I am daring myself to continue this habit with the following ask:

Would you consider sharing a review of this book on your favourite online retailer?

Exhale... I did it!

Thank you, and I can't wait to hear from you.

Cheering you on,

JANE

(P.S. I would love to connect with you. Instagram is where I hang out. You can find me at @TheJaneWilson and @BeginnerPoleDancing. Be sure to say hi!)